Helene Andreu holds a master's degree in dance education from Teachers College at Columbia University and has considerable experience as a dancer, dance teacher, and choreographer. She teaches dance at New York City Community College and the Stuyvesant Adult Education School.

J

jazz dance
an adult beginner's guide

Helene Andreu

A SPECTRUM BOOK

Prentice-Hall, Inc.   Englewood Cliffs, New Jersey 07632

Library of Congress Cataloging in Publication Data

Andreu, Helene.
    Jazz dance.

    "A Spectrum Book."
    Discography: p.
    Bibliography: p.
    Includes index.
    1. Jazz dance.   I. Title.
GV1753.A56   793.3   82-3738
ISBN 0-13-509968-4   AACR2
ISBN 0-13-509950-1 (pbk.)

This book is available at a special discount when ordered in bulk quantities. Contact Prentice-Hall, Inc., General Publishing Division, Special Sales, Englewood Cliffs, N.J. 07632.

A SPECTRUM BOOK

10 9 8 7 6 5 4 3 2 1

Printed in the United States of America

Editorial/production supervision
and interior design by Cyndy Lyle Rymer
Page layout by Diane Heckler-Koromhas

Manufacturing buyer Christine Johnston
Cover design by Judith Kazdym Leeds

ISBN 0-13-509968-4

ISBN 0-13-509950-1 (PBK.)

Prentice-Hall International, Inc., *London*
Prentice-Hall of Australia Pty. Limited, *Sydney*
Prentice-Hall of Canada Inc., *Toronto*
Prentice-Hall of India Private Limited, *New Delhi*
Prentice-Hall of Japan, Inc., *Tokyo*
Prentice-Hall of Southeast Asia, Pte. Ltd., *Singapore*
Whitehall Books Limited, *Wellington, New Zealand*
Editora Prentice-Hall do Brasil Ltda., *Rio de Janeiro*

contents

preface

This book should prove a valuable guide to anyone interested in learning more about jazz dance. Whether your interest is primarily in doing it yourself or simply in understanding more about it, you will get enjoyment from the many basic jazz walks, simpler steps, and arm movements, which are presented in clearly written explanations with sequential stick figure illustrations that mirror-image the description in the text. Specific counts are given in the descriptions of the steps, and these are shown in the illustrations to provide ease in execution and to assist you to add the syncopation of rhythm that is basic to jazz dance.

You will enjoy using these basic steps again in the more intricate combinations given in the second half of the book. Included are references to the places in the book where you can look up the steps used in the combination, if you need to refresh your memory, as well as photographs for visual reminders.

Suggestions are given for putting together your own routines utilizing the material presented in the book. The results of several student group choreography projects will show the variety of routines possible by groups or individuals through the addition of their own ideas, while using the same basic steps.

You will enjoy the increased muscle tone, strength, and flexibility acquired by doing the warm-up and isolation exercises in *Jazz Dance*. There are useful reminders regarding relaxation, alignment, and what to watch out for in order to avoid common problems in the execution of the exercises.

The historical background and evolution of jazz dance is presented with all the varied influences of primitive jazz, social dance, Latin dance, tap, ballet, and modern dance. The steps given in *Jazz Dance* often have notes showing the influence of some of the other dance forms on its development. This, together with a clearly written description of the similarities and differences between ballet, modern, and jazz dance, should aid the reader in doing the jazz steps more correctly through a better comprehension of their background.

Chapter 1 gives the reader a background on jazz music and dance from which to better understand the subject. Chapter 2 offers ideas for home or class practice. From then on the reader is carefully guided, verbally and visually, through the warm-ups, isolations, simple steps, turns, and arm movements to the more complex combinations and routines. Everything is done with concern for the reader through detailed explanations and visual step-by-step sketches. Art and sheet music covers related to the subject are provided; there are also dance photographs interspersed throughout the book—you are encouraged to try to identify the steps shown in the photographs as you read the book. The reader is also encouraged to vary the arm movements, to add his or her ideas to the jazz walks, and to use what has been learned and make it unique by putting together individual routines. The influence of jazz music on the evolution of jazz dance is stressed. A discography is included listing numerous long-playing jazz records and some of the selections to be found in each. Sheet music covers can be seen in Chapter 1 with notes about the music or about the Broadway show represented. A comprehensive bibliography should aid the reader in finding out more about his or her new found interest. An interest in jazz dance will provide the reader with an outlet that can be stimulating and refreshing, not only for the body, but also to the eye, the ear, and the mind.

I wish to thank my family, friends, and Mary Kennan of Prentice-Hall for their support, ideas, and cooperation while I was writing this book; especially my father for proofreading it. I also wish to thank my dance students for letting me take photographs; likewise all my teachers and students, whose ideas, ways of doing things, and questions and answers helped to make this book what it is.

Permission to use photographs of artwork and illustrations from books and booklets was granted by The Museum of Modern Art and National Academy of Design, New York; Hampton Institute, Virginia; Fabbri Editori, Italy, and the Government of India Tourist Office.

Permission to use sheet music covers was granted by Warner Bros., Inc.; Shapiro, Bernstein and Co., Inc.; Williamson Music, Inc.; Unichappell Music, Inc.; Chappell and Co., Inc.; and Southwest Amusement Corp. Photographs of Ms. Andreu are by Clotilde; photographs of sheet music covers and groups as well as the original sketches were done by the author.

I appreciate the great help and service obtained from Sam Ash Music Store; Patelson's Music House; American Society of Composers and Publishers (ASCAP); Broadcast Music Inc. (BMI); The Film Center, New York; Dumont Camera Corp., New York; Foto Depot #2, Brooklyn; all the marvelous photocopy places in Flatbush; and New York City Technical College for its extensive selection of books on music and art, which facilitated my research.

1
an introduction to jazz dance

I told a friend that I was writing a book about jazz dance, and he said, "That's great. I saw the movie *Oklahoma* on TV; I really liked the dancing; that dream sequence with the cowboy dance and the bawdy ladies flinging their skirts around and showing their legs—now that's jazz, isn't it?"

"No, not really," I said. "The cowboy scene is modern ballet with quite a bit of Americana for flavoring, and the bawdy ladies were doing a cancan, which is originally French, has lots of skirts showing and some legs, but no pelvic isolations, and was at one time considered very risque."

"Well," he said, "then what about *West Side Story*?"

"Oh, that's predominantly jazz," I answered. "There is a feeling of stepping down into the floor rather than up into the air in many of the dance sequences; knees were bent; lots of hip and shoulder isolations as well as syncopation of rhythm could be found in the movements."

"I see," he said, "but what's that feller's name—oh, yes, Jerome Robbins—doesn't he choreograph for the New York City Ballet Company also?"

"Sure he does," I replied, "and there he does anything from a jazz ballet to a more classical ballet or modern ballet. And so do lots of other choreographers either on TV, in Broadway shows, movies, or concerts."

"So, how do I know what I'm seeing," my friend asked, "if

they have jazz and modern dance in a ballet company and then ballet, modern, and jazz in a Broadway show?"

"Oh, there are still more varieties of dance and movement that get mixed into these," I said. "There are ethnic and folk—all the Americana, East Indian, Afro, Afro-Haitian, Spanish Flamenco, Russian, Greek, Italian, English, and so on, as well as tap and precision line, social dance, and acrobatics. Nowadays, any kind of dance can be mixed in with any other. There is a great deal of intermingling of all dance areas."

"Fine," my friend said, "now just tell me how I can spot a jazz dance when I'm watching dance, and how I can tell if it's ballet, modern, or jazz. Who knows," he added, "I might want to take a class myself. Those dancers look like they're having fun. But, if I don't know what it is I'm watching, if I like it and want to study it, I won't know what to study."

At that point my bus came and I never did finish my explanation, so I will finish it now and hope my friend reads the book.

FIGURE 1-1 "Lucky To Be Me" from *On the Town,* a musical based on a story line similar to the ballet *Fancy Free* (Jerome Robbins)—about sailors "out on the town"—that was choreographed by Robbins to music by Leonard Bernstein; both later did *West Side Story* (originally published by Witmark & Sons, © 1944). Copyright © 1944 by Warner Bros. Inc. Copyright renewed, all rights reserved. Used by permission.

Dance is as old as the human race, and the more one knows about its history, the more expertly one can tell from where certain types of movements in jazz, ballet, or modern dance originated, and how they are related. Somebody did not get up one bright morning and say, "Well, let's start a new dance called *jazz*." Jazz just evolved; the precursors of jazz dance had no idea that it would evolve, any more than we can say for sure today where it is going. What happens in dance is related to what happens to people, with changes in social customs and historical events. Of the three—ballet, modern, and jazz—ballet is the oldest, and jazz is the youngest in the sense of being the latest to be accepted as an area of dance that is worth seeing, writing about, choreographing, performing, and studying. Since this book is about jazz dance, let us start with a brief outline of the characteristics of ballet and modern dance; if you compare these with jazz, you should be able to tell the difference and to see their influence in a jazz dance.

CLASSICAL BALLET

Ballet is a form of theater dancing for spectators, more than 325 years old, which developed gradually from folk dances to court dances to theater dance with a tradition of style, technique, and terminology known all over the world. It developed principally in Italy, France, and Russia, and its terminology is French.

The early development and organization of ballet was mainly by men (their writing, notation, and choreography), but the starring roles more often belonged to the women, whose technique increased as their skirts became shorter and lighter, allowing them more freedom of movement.

The characteristics of classical ballet (and these show up in ballet jazz—a mixture of ballet and jazz dance) are:

Use of turnout of the legs.
Pointed feet extending the line of the leg to the toes.
A noble bearing (Louis XIV of France, who did much to promote ballet, took daily lessons for over 20 years, around 1620).
Charm and grace.
A look of effortlessness and ease in execution.
Fluid, rounded arms.
Lightness.
A highly evolved technique that has been tested over the years and has developed discipline, strength, flexibility, speed, grace, and style.

an introduction to jazz dance

Long lines with taut muscles in high extensions.

Multiple turns done on a small base, demi-pointe, or in toe shoes for the women, or in the air.

Defiance of gravity shown in spectacular high leaps done with apparent effortlessness, and intricate lifts by the male dancer, giving the ballerina the appearance of weightlessness.

Use of soft ballet slippers for ease in pointing the feet.

Development of a special toe shoe with leather shank and glue to stiffen the satin toe section and to enable the women to rise high on their toes.

An ethereal look as in the romantic ballets. (Anyone with sore feet in toe shoes would have to either think bright or ethereal thoughts or take off the toe shoes as the modern dancers did.)

At present, ballet companies offer a wide selection of dance styles, from original classical ballets dating back more than 125 years, to contemporary ballets with extensive use of jazz isolations (see Chapter 4) and syncopated rhythms (see Index), to modern ballets or dances by modern dance choreographers. Some of these choreographers have their own modern dance companies, but they also enjoy working with ballet companies. However, their dances may have a slightly different look here because the dancers' training is more ballet oriented, with an emphasis on line rather than on volume; or on height of jumps rather than on space covered; or on effortlessness of execution rather than on making obvious the effort expended. Check the Bibliography and your library for books about ballet and modern dance.

MODERN DANCE

Born around the turn of the century, modern dance sprang out of a need for some other kind of theatrical dance besides ballet. It started in Germany, but the bulk of its development has been in the United States, or by Americans in Europe, greatly through the work of very determined women in its early years. They also greatly changed the acceptable attire of dancers to no corsets, no shoes, then shorter dresses, tunics, leotards, and even partial or complete nudity (not too usual, however) in a dance atmosphere that was *not* hard sell. It was each choreographer's unique manner of creating dances that made modern dance important, and thus it has as many characteristics as there are responses to the need for movement.

Starting with early modern dance and going on to avant-garde modern dance, the characteristics (which show up again in modern jazz—a mixture of modern and jazz dance) are:

Highly individualized approach to dance movement.

Use of everyday movements, such as combing one's hair, and natural movements, such as running or walking.

Extends from a very theatrical use of lights, costumes, and music to stark realism.

Angular lines, flexed feet, and no turnout were the earlier characteristics that developed as a reaction against ballet artificiality. (Modern dancers, generally heavier than ballet dancers, did not do ballet-type warm-ups; they did flex feet and elbows.)

A counterreaction or a return to ballet technique and positions, but with variations—use of some ballet steps, positions, and arms, but without a turnout, perhaps with a flexed wrist, and so on. (They did do ballet-type warm-ups, and they flexed feet and elbows at times, and they became more slender.)

Use of fall and recovery.

Use of contraction and release of the torso.

Making no effort to hide the tension and effort expended in a given movement.

Locomotor movements using unusual parts of the body rather than the usual two feet (such as the side of the body, together with one elbow and one foot).

Both a dramatization of inner conflicts and a dehumanization of movement in dance.

Movement for itself rather than to convey a message or story.

Use of ethnic dance movements, derived from traditional folk dances or typical movements of a people—East Indian, Americana (cowboys, pioneers).

An attempt to use movements natural to the individual's body, not harmful to it (and as everyone is not built the same, it varies).

Use of bare feet, modern dance sandals, or more recently, sneakers.

Use of irregular meter in music; extensive use of contemporary American music; use of music and sounds created by the choreographer, including electronic music.

Doing a movement with the least possible amount of tension or expenditure of energy.

Use of chance as a method of choreography, to aid in freeing the choreographer from his or her usual method of working.

Use of multimedia—slides and film, as well as poetry readings or vocal sounds, along with live dance movement.

Interest in spectator-performer interaction and happenings.

Defiance of gravity in off-center balances and turns, and also walking on walls with the assistance of ropes and equipment, in some avant garde modern dance routines.

Intellectualization and problem-solving, in which a choreographer sets some sort of a problem dealing with space, time, pattern of movement—circles, lines—and attempts to solve it in a dance, with or without the spectators being made aware of this fact.

Use of everyday gestures, sports, or work skill movements.

Use of nondancers either alone or together with dancers.

Present-day modern dance, being very individualistic, can include any of the above (but not all of them in any one dance); it may also include use of ballet technique (frowned upon by earlier founders of modern dance), as well as jazz and some occasional tap. If you can't tell what a dance is—ballet, jazz, or modern, it is probably modern dance, since this form allows the most diversity of ideas to come into its presentation. At its most avant-garde, modern dance could be called "anything goes."

JAZZ DANCE

This dance form is younger than ballet or modern dance, at least in being recognized as a theatrical form of dance throughout the world. Like modern dance and tap, the greater part of its theatrical development has been in the United States. It is a truly American dance form and reflects the origins, history, economics, creativity, and music of its people in its form.

Jazz dance has its base in the folk dances of the African people, who had a dance for every aspect of life. It was not a theatrical dance then, since the entire community took part. The characteristics of African folk dance are even now characteristics of jazz dance as a whole, and more specifically of *primitive jazz,* so called because it came out of the movements found in the early folk dances of African heritage. These movements are:

Bent knees—the body center is closer to the ground than is usual in everyday posture.

Isolation of body parts—hips, shoulders, head, ribcage.

Syncopated rhythms of movement.

Two and three rhythms going on at a time in one body.

Use of the entire body rather than just legs and arms as a means of expressing oneself in movement. The expression and movement ripple out from the body center.

The difference between primitive jazz and the original African folk dance is that the latter had a purpose in the culture's society, whereas

FIGURE 1-2 Toulouse-Lautrec's poster of Jane Avril was painted specifically to advertise her appearance as solo cancan dancer at the Jardin de Paris when the cancan was at its peak. Lautrec painted many dances of that era—Loie Fuller, La Goulue, and Jane Avril. Like millions now as well as then, the artist was attracted not only by the dancing but by the whole effect of the clothes, hats, and lovely blend of colors chosen by the dancers for their costumes, especially Jane Avril. *Jane Avril au Jardin de Paris*, Henri de Toulouse-Lautrec, c. 1893; 51¼ x 37½ in. Courtesy of Fabbri Editori, Milan, Italy.

primitive jazz is made up of movements taken out of context from those original folk dances and rechoreographed into a routine by the teacher or choreographer (unless he or she states that it is actually an authentic African folk dance).

The last characteristic listed—use of the whole body including the ribcage and hips as a means of dance expression—was frowned upon by European cultures. Although many religions include dance as a part of the ceremony, the Christian church banned dancing altogether from ceremonies after the twelfth century. It was viewed as being too worldly, since it did involve the human body, and was believed to take human thoughts away from God. Except for some peasant dances that had a few hip sways (covered by long heavy skirts), the hips and torsos did not move in European dances, only the shoulders, arms, and legs. The exception seems to have been the classical Spanish dance, with the Moorish influence of undulating hips, but even those costumes seem to have been fuller and less revealing years ago than the more formfitting costumes worn by contemporary Spanish dancers. A French dance that was considered very vulgar and risque—the cancan—had lots of skirt and leg raising (high kicks and splits), but no wiggles (See Figure 1-2). It was, nevertheless, not a dance for ladies or gentlemen.

In America, Calvinists and some other Puritan religions banned dancing altogether. And that was the attitude confronting African slaves when they were brought to the New World. Their dances were looked at from a European point of view, and although the Americans may have enjoyed the dances, they did not accept them, at least not at first. But as customs, clothes, and society changed, so did the attitude toward dance, and dances which use all parts of the body are now very acceptable in all forms of ballet, modern, and jazz. Then, too, peoples' attitudes toward their bodies have changed, as has the attitude of many Christian churches toward dance; several churches now offer modern dance as a part of their service (liturgical dance), and many Catholic schools offer dance in the curriculum. (The Shakers and Holy Rollers are two of the few Christian sects in early America always to have had religious dancing.)

HISTORY OF JAZZ DANCE IN AMERICA

The African slaves who were brought to the Americas—the West Indies, Cuba, Panama, Haiti, and the United States—brought their dances with them. Their dance, so great a part of their heritage, survived, adapted, and took on a slightly different form in different areas. In Afro-Haitian jazz can be found many movements taken from the religious dancing in that area. From Cuba, Haiti, Panama, and South America eventually came the cha-cha, mambo, pachanga, merengue, samba, and the conga, which were then adapted, "cleaned up," popularized in the United States, and taught by ballroom couples such as Vernon and Irene Castle and Tony and Sally De Marco. The dances that developed form the basis of the movements found in *Latin jazz* (see Fig. 1-3).

In the United States, blacks adapted and added to the Irish foot rhythms their own free and easy arm swings and body movements that were not found in Irish clog dancing, and gradually there evolved *American Tap* and *Jazz Tap*. The European waltz, infused with the rhythm, artistry, and humor of black Americans, quickly became the Charleston, Black Bottom, Big Apple, the two-step, varsity drag, mooch, the shimmy (see Fig. 1-4), and later, trucking, the shag, Suzie-Q, jitterbug, and twist.

FIGURE 1-3 "Papa Loves Mambo." In the 1940s and 50s, many Latin dances and music with a new sense of rhythm were introduced in the United States and became popular both on the ballroom floor and on Broadway and television. *Damn Yankees* was one of the Broadway musicals (choreography by Bob Fosse) that featured a mambo sequence. As with many social dances with an influence on jazz dance, the appearance of a mambo in a show intensified its popularity in the ballroom and all danced the mambo eagerly. Copyright © 1954 by Shapiro, Bernstein & Co., used by permission.

Went to a dance with my sister Kate,
Everyone there said she danced so great.
I realized a thing or two,
Then I got wise to something new,
I look'd at Kate, she was in a trance
And then I knew it was in her dance.
All the boys are going wild
Just over Katie's dancing style.

Wish I could shimmy like my sister Kate,
She shivers like the jelly on a plate;
My mammy wanted to know last night,
Why all the boys treat Sister Kate so nice,
Every boy in our neighborhood
Knows that she can shimmy and it's understood.
I know I'm late but I'll be up to date,
When I can shimmy like my sister Kate.*

FIGURE 1-4 "I Wish I Could Shimmy Like My Sister Kate." This was one of the popular tunes of the 1920s, when millions were doing the shimmy. Copyright © 1919 by Armand J. Piron, copyright renewed 1946 by Oxana Piron. Copyright assigned to Jerry Vogel Music Co., Inc. Used by permission of Jerry Vogel Music Co., Inc.

Some other dances—with very descriptive names—were the turkey trot, chicken scratch, monkey, and the bunny hug. (The fox-trot, however, which was livelier then than today, was originally named after Harry Fox, who trotted onstage in 1913 at the beginning of his act and got a dance named after him!) These social dances that came from African animal dances (dances that resembled animal movements) and those that developed from the waltz found their way into theatrical jazz dances as *jazz derived from early social dances*. A dance in a present-day musical dealing with the 1920s does not have to duplicate exactly the dances of the 1920s as long as there are enough basic movements from that era to represent it well.

*Lyrics reprinted by permission of Jerry Vogel Music Co., Inc. Copyright ©1919 by Armand J. Piron, copyright renewed 1946 by Oxana Piron. Copyright assigned to Jerry Vogel Music Co., Inc.

By the end of the nineteenth century, social dance had won acceptance in America, but theatrical dance was slower in gaining recognition. Performers were generally looked at with disfavor. Several people in the audience walked out when Isadora Duncan, the famous modern dancer, shocked them by dancing in bare arms and legs. And she, in turn, although not willing to be bound by conventions herself, considered the new music and the dance it inspired coarse and vulgar; she disapproved of the slightly clad chorus girls!

Blacks in early America continued dancing to entertain themselves, or their masters during slavery, either with new forms of original dances or by adapting the dances of white people if they were not allowed to perform their own. Slaves were considered more valuable if they had musical or dance aptitude, so naturally this encouraged improvisation of music and imitation and adaptation of the dances they saw (see Fig. 1-5). Little by little the songs and dances of black people did appear on stage, but blacks themselves were represented in minstrel shows by the white man in cork blackface, usually depicting the black as a comic, grotesque character, or as a dandy. "Daddy" Rice, a white performer (1820s), was well known for his rendition of the "Jim Crow," an Afro-American dance.

The dances in minstrel shows were all fairly authentic versions of black dances—the buck dance, the pigeon wing—as seen by white people on plantations when the slaves were asked or forced to entertain white owners and guests, or on holidays, or in contests (between slaves of different masters) of jigs, or cakewalks where couples "walked" against each other with intricate steps and the winner "took the cake." (See Fig. 1-11) The movements might also be taken from imitations of work positions of black people, but they were shown on stage as caricatures. The dance may have been "authentic" as seen by white people, but the outcome depended on whom they looked at. "Daddy" Rice was said to have imitated the Jim Crow dance as done by a lame black man named Jim Crow, who apparently danced excellently in spite of his lameness. The movements seemed natural, but at the same time somehow grotesque due to his handicap. Today there are still several jazz steps that look like descendants of this kind of dance and that could easily be done by someone with one lame leg. (If you ever do have a really sore leg, and you are cold and have not done any dance warm-ups, try a few dance steps that you know in front of a mirror. They will come out looking different than usual. But you may like the way they look; you might

an introduction to jazz dance

FIGURE 1-5 *The Banjo Lesson* by Henry C. Tanner, c. 1893. Oil on canvas, 48 × 35 in. An aptitude in music and dance was considered an asset in a slave during the years slavery existed. The banjo was the usual accompaniment for dance in minstrel shows. Reprinted by courtesy of the Hampton Institute, Hampton, Virginia.

not have thought of that step otherwise. Remember the step and try it again, if you can, when you feel well; it may not be as easy then.)

From the "all-white" minstrel shows, gradually a change took place, and a few black men were allowed to perform on stage—but only in an all black cast for audiences that were all black. Between 1863-93 black minstrel shows became very popular. Juba, a performer who was well liked by both black and white audiences, was the exception; he did perform in a white minstrel show with three white men and even toured Europe with them. Master Juba was the stage name adopted by William Henry Lane, born a free black, from *juba,* the name of a black dance. He did specialties of his own and also imitated all the reputed dancers of his day in the steps for which they were famous. In turn, white minstrel performers imitated Juba. In 1866, after three challenges were danced between black Master Juba and white Master Diamond, a minstrel show performer who excelled in black dance, Juba won and thereupon joined the three white minstrels, receiving "top billing," which was very unusual.

So, a lot of dance material found in minstrel shows was of authentic black origin. Or more precisely, the dances were white and black imitations of black adaptations of whatever dances white and black people were doing, or "authentic black material," which is why it is complicated to trace a particular step to its origin. But if you know something about the background, you might be able to guess the origin of a step. For example, a *flea hop* step *could* have been a black's adaptation of the Irish jig (prevalent in early America), since the flea hop is bent over slightly, has a loose arm swing, and a flat-footed slide sideways instead of a true Irish hopping movement.

Some of the dances performed in the minstrel shows were snake hips, camel walk, fish bones, buzzard lope, ball the jack, grapevine twist, and walking jaw bones. A few found their way into our *rock and roll jazz* and *disco jazz,* and some dances of today have names that are just as descriptive—bus stop, hitch hiker—as the ones that existed back then. They form a part of theatrical *jazz from recent social dances* or rock and roll jazz and disco jazz (see Fig. 1-10). These later dances are considered related to our earlier ones. The plantation couple dances performed by slaves had body wiggles and yet no body contact, much like the disco dances of the 1960s. Both were done in the "challenge" position—facing each other, but not touching one's partner, which is the same position found in the Charleston. In the 1960s, psychologists were quick to point out the significance of the challenge position in our society, usually all bad—the breakdown of social and family ties. A few, however, did say that it was the need to be in a group, yet with the feeling of being able to do one's own thing. Others said it was not so; everyone ended up doing the same thing but separately.

After the Civil War, theatrical extravaganzas and "leg shows" (legomania) started to appear. The Prohibition party began in 1869; the Women's Christian Temperance Union was formed, and it endorsed women's suffrage in the 1880s. Blacks began to move north. At the beginning of the twentieth century, clubs in Harlem, such as the Cotton Club, attracted attention for their jazz music especially, and also for the dances that were an outcome of its rhythms: the mooch, shimmy, trucking, lindy hop, and jitterbug; these gradually became popular with both black and white people.

Jazz music made great strides—first through the blues, spirituals, and work songs of southern blacks; the slave work songs with their melancholy intensity had an influence on blues and even on ragtime. The slight lowering of certain pitches in the singing is what produces the melancholy shade, or "blue" note, in the music— the slightly flattened thirds and sevenths of the major scale and also the use of the pentatonic scale. All this black music, together with the influence of French and Spanish popular songs, became ragtime, which absorbed the characteristic rhythms of black marching bands, that is, of shifting the accent from the strong to the weak beat. That in turn can be traced back to the foot stomping and hand clapping found in southern Methodist revival meetings, rather than to West African music, which has more complicated rhythms. In New Orleans, bands marched for any and all reasons—advertisements, deaths, holidays, whatever. If two bands met at an intersection, they battled it out in music until one of them was declared the winner. These bands were very popular (remember there was no TV at the time).

Marches were very popular, too. They were used to dance the two-step, which replaced the ever-popular waltz. If you syncopated a march you had ragtime. (Syncopation is an effect of uneven rhythm resulting from deliberately shifting the accent from the expected beat by either a slight hesitation, or a pause, or by placing the accent on a weak beat or an offbeat. This effect is increased when played against a regularly accented beat. The syncopation or the regular pulse can be in either the melody or the bass. In ragtime the bass has the regular beat.) Ragtime gradually became composed—written— music and lost some of its improvisational quality, but the other forms of jazz music allowed for a great deal of spontaneous improvisation in performance. The basic rhythm of ragtime evolved from that of a two-step or cakewalk, and later became the grizzly bear, bunny hug, turkey trot, and Texas Tommy. These evolved into the fast music and dances of the 1920s—the one-step, lindy hop, Charleston, and Black Bottom.

Early ragtime musicians were improvisers and used no written music. Their ragtime was characterized by a very syncopated (irregular rhythm) melody played against a bass with a regularly accented beat. This music, with its improvisation and lack of written notes, was not acceptable in "good society" at first, but it flourished in Storyville, a legal red light district of New Orleans, and other places of like repute, until Storyville was closed by the government in 1918 and the musicians moved north to Harlem clubs and dance halls in New York by way of Chicago (see Fig. 1-6).

Ragtime was popularized by the white musicians who hastened its progress in the dance halls of the nation and adapted the jazz style into what became known as New Orleans Dixieland jazz; the Original Dixieland Jazz Band recorded its first tune, "Tiger Rag." Jazz swept the nation and influenced the dancing public of the early twentieth century. Soon it became swing, rock and roll, and bebop,

FIGURE 1-6 "Roxie" (music and lyrics by Kander and Ebb) from the hit musical *Chicago*, which was based on a dramatic Ginger Rogers movie of the early 1940s. *Chicago*, directed and choreographed by Bob Fosse, was full of cabaret-type numbers, music of the 1920s, and the Chicago jazz style.Copyright © 1974 & 1975 by Unichappell Music, Inc. & Kander-Ebb, Inc. Unichappell Music, Inc., Administrator. International copyright secured. All Rights Reserved. Used by permission.

the only music to reach the ears of the younger generation, and it greatly helped to promote jazz dance since jazz music is what people danced to in the ballroom and on the stage and what they heard on the radio and saw on TV and film.

Just as jazz music became of great importance in America, so did jazz dance, and new dance styles evolved to suit the big band jazz music. Jazz also went abroad with the American military in the 1940s, and the latest jazz music and dances became popular over there, too. This was the time when jazz dance was strongest—in the social dance scene with the lindy, jitterbug, rock and roll, twist and then disco. Radio programs such as "Rock 'Round the Clock" and "Make Believe Ballroom" helped to promote the latest jazz music and dances in the 1950s. On television, "American Bandstand," with 25 years on the air by 1977, had even won an older audience through its fresh presentation of the lindy and rock and roll dances as three generations of teenagers and adults watched and listened; skirts for the girls and jackets for the boys were a must for those in the audience since they would later get up to participate in the dancing and be seen by the television audiences.

As for the name *jazz,* opinions differ concerning where it originated. Some theories were presented to readers of the *New York Dramatic Mirror* in 1919. It could have been named after a player in a spasm band (a popular type of band made up of washboards and homemade instruments); he was called Jasper, or Jas, for short, and at first the bands did spell the music as *jass.* Another version is that his name was Charles, abbreviated Chas, and mispronounced or misread as Chaz or Jaz. Or, it came from Razz's Band and became Jazz Band. Or, again it may really have been of African derivation. However, Tom Brown took his band to Chicago from New Orleans in 1915 and used the word *jass* (later to become *jazz*) to identify the music they played—Brown's Dixieland Jass Band—and the name *jazz* stuck. In 1919 a popular song was called "Take Me to the World of Jazz" (Wendling and Kalmar). Now that the music had a name, it became easier to identify it as jazz music and the dances people did to it as jazz dance (which is probably why social dances done to jazz music—shimmy, twist, lindy, rock and roll—are considered jazz, whereas those that developed before jazz music—gavotte, waltz, polka—never came into the domain of jazz).

Meanwhile, on the theatrical side, about the time of the famous Harlem clubs, Bill Robinson, Earl "Snake Hips" Jones, the Nicholas Brothers, and Avon Long were acclaimed for their dancing. Black dance was becoming popular in such revues as *Shuffle Along* (1921), with "I'm Just Wild About Harry"—music by Eubie

Blake—and *Blackbirds* (1926 and 1928) with high kicks and the Charleston, and also the tap "staircase dance" made famous by Bill Robinson to "Doin' The New Low Down." The famous names in jazz for some time were predominantly, but not always, men.

Electricity had been used to light the stages gradually in the United States since 1883, when Steele MacKaye first used it to light an American stage. Loie Fuller, one of the early American modern dancers, had gained a reputation in Europe, mainly due to her imaginative use of lights and colors. At a time when electricity had barely been discovered, she traveled with a crew of more than 40 electricians to light her act, and she set a precedent in creative lighting design.

Chaperones were passé; automobiles were becoming increasingly popular with young adults. The Vatican condemned the turkey trot (with the pumping arm down at the side); Boston banned first the tango and then the cheek-to-cheek dancing found in the hug-like close dance position of the popular grizzly bear. Skirts were getting shorter. The talkies appeared about 1927; the stock market crashed, and immediately followed the Great Depression.

The Jazz Singer with Al Jolson was the beginning of movie musicals. They soon were being produced in a very elaborate, grandiose manner, even more so than the famous stage productions by Ziegfeld or the *Earl Carroll Vanities* or *George White's Scandals* stage shows. The first such movies were glorified vaudeville and extravaganzas, many of them with the renowned Busby Berkeley's great imagination in staging effects (a reputation he had already acquired staging live shows by Ziegfeld and Carroll). Soon came all the great Fred Astaire-Ginger Rogers movie musicals, such as *Top Hat* and *Swingtime,* with excellent creative tap, ballroom, and jazz tap, choreographed by Hermes Pan and Fred Astaire, with great music by Gershwin, Berlin, Porter, Youmans, and Kern. Tickets for movies were far less expensive than theater tickets and films were seen by millions. The movies presented imaginative ideas, great music, dances, and songs, with beautiful settings, costumes and far away lands. The movies flourished and theatrical presentations went into a decline. However, there were, and continued to be, many excellent movies that were based on original Broadway shows (see Fig. 1-7), some with the same stars, choreographers, and production numbers, and some very different from the original stage productions.

The black musical, recognized for its superior dancing in the 1920s, did not make a comeback until the 1970s with *Bubbling Brown Sugar* (see Fig. 1-8), *The Wiz, Ain't Misbehavin,* and *Eubie* (with music by Eubie Blake), although there had been an occasional

an introduction to jazz dance

FIGURE 1-7 "Grant Avenue" from the movie musical *Flower Drum Song*. The original Broadway show (1958) was directed by Gene Kelly, and the movie (1961) was under the direction of Henry Koster. Choreographer Carol Haney created many jazzy production numbers that were slick, well executed, and well liked in a smoothly flowing show. The movie, choreography by Hermes Pan, retained the sharp execution of the Broadway production numbers. The plot was based on a novel by C.Y. Lee about San Francisco's Chinatown. Copyright © 1958 by Richard Rodgers & Oscar Hammerstein II; Williamson Music, Inc., owner of publication and allied rights throughout the Western Hemisphere and Japan. International copyright secured. All Rights Reserved. Used by permission.

FIGURE 1-8 One of the many excellent black musicals of the 1970s, *Bubbling Brown Sugar* was produced in 1976. The title song was by Danny Holgate, Lillian Lopez and Emme Kemp; choreography by Billy Wilson (jazz and tap), with other music by Duke Ellington and others. The story line was based on Harlem life from 1920 to 1940. Copyright © 1975 & 1976 by Soundboosters, Inc. and Truckin' Music Corp. Chappell & Co., Inc., Administrator. International copyright secured. All Rights Reserved. Used by permission.

show before then. All of the productions in the 1970s had excellent jazz tap and jazz dance.

Jazz dancing is considered to have taken some sort of a definite form, or one that was recognized and taught, about 1915–20. Before that time, there were no choreographers for shows; there were minstrel shows, then vaudeville shows and extravaganzas, then musical comedies, with entertainers or soloists responsible for improvising or preparing their own routines. The chorus girls were hired for their looks rather than for dance technique. Instead of choreographers, there were directors of the ensemble, responsible for getting the chorus girls into some sort of dance shape rather quickly, using precision line formations and interesting and creative groupings that did not overtax their abilities, but did fill the space. Kicks and simpler steps known to everyone were used and reused as late as the 1930s.

The ensemble did unison dancing and singing, but the stars had private coaches, whom they paid for themselves. The coaches carefully taught the stars their routines; the stars performed them; the routines were tailored to fit the exact requirements and talents of the star. The public assumed that the star had personally prepared the routine, but coaches accepted this; they had been paid for creating routines and made their reputations in the trade by the stars' excellence. One such coach was Buddy Bradley. He created routines specifically for Clifton Webb, Pat Rooney, Mae West, and others. Bradley was inspired by music; he bought many jazz records, listened to them, and let the syncopation of the music lead him in his choreography, as many choreographers have done before and after him. As shows began to require better technique of the dancers, the traditional jazz movements that had been learned by observation were now beginning to be taken apart into isolations (movements in which you isolate and move each individual part of the body separately), walks, and simple steps for class use, and then reassembled creatively by choreographers into dance routines. Gradually, other forms of dance were added—steps, turns, jumps, and so on—to suit individual taste, ability, and national background; and that is how jazz dance grew.

THE GROWTH OF MUSICAL COMEDY

In the 1930s, ballet and modern dance in America started to gain in importance, due to a renewed interest in visiting foreign ballet companies and to many determined founders of modern dance, such

an introduction to jazz dance

as Ruth St. Denis, Ted Shawn, and others, who opened schools throughout the country. The result was more well-trained dancers than ever before, which in turn probably caused musical comedy to go through many phases.

Audiences had already seen tap and precision line dancing (like the Tiller Girls, with uniform lines and high kicks), and now ballet and modern dance appeared. The shows of the time usually had a singing ensemble with excellent pear-shaped tones and a separate dancing group. There was very little individualization of chorus members. They were dressed in identical costumes and did not represent different real people on stage. (Today they are usually given character names in the program notes. If they are in identical costumes it is often as part of a chorus in a show within a show, as in *A Chorus Line* and *42nd Street*.) The chorus usually appeared to open the show, to allow for latecomers in the audience to be seated, and to assure everyone that beautiful girls were part of the performance. They were not a dramatic part of the story, just a diversion.

With ballet came the need for excellent technique and training and choreographers to set the routines. Improvisation was out and technique was in, at least in order to be able to do someone else's choreography. George Balanchine choreographed *On Your Toes* (1936), and that's where it was—on the toes, not even ballet in soft shoes as today—and it also included a jazz ballet number (in street shoes, not toe shoes).

Next came modern dance on the musical comedy stage, with such choreographers as Charles Weidman, Helen Tamaris, Hanya Holm, Jack Cole, and Agnes de Mille. And it brought a liberating influence in groupings and movements, as well as a freeing of constrictions concerning what a dance should be. Agnes de Mille was especially influential in this area. The dream ballet in *Oklahoma* and the bereaved woman's dance in *Brigadoon* were remarkable for their impact and success in a musical comedy. An interest in East Indian dance also developed, as part of the modern dance phase (see Fig. 1-9) either due to the influence of the modern dancers' use of these movements, or to the storyline of the musicals, or to the allure of exotic lands.

All of these influences found their way into Hindu jazz, modern jazz, and balletic jazz, and musical comedy production in general. Jack Cole, who choreographed *Alive and Kicking,* had a background in Denishawn and Humphrey-Weidman dance styles, which were innovative modern dance techniques, and also used motifs and ideas based on ethnic backgrounds—East Indian, Americana, and so on. Cole's choreography showed this influence. He was

Figure 1-9 Indian dancer from "Heritage of Dance," courtesy of the Government of India Tourist Office. The use of intricate head and hand movements in Indian dance, which is depicted here, fascinated modern dancers such as Ruth St. Denis. Such movements were used by dancers wherever they appeared—in burlesque, vaudeville, and even on the concert stage. These dancers also taught the intricate hand and head movements in their schools and influenced many future choreographers, jazz teachers, and jazz dancers, among others. These types of movements later appeared in a wide variety of Broadway shows such as *Alive and Kicking* (Jack Cole, choreographer), *The King and I* (Jerome Robbins, choreographer), and numerous other Broadway shows where the dancing required very precise hand movements, such as *The Magic Show* (Grover Dale, choreographer).

remarkably creative in his integration of East Indian movement, Latin motifs, and jazz rhythms.

At this time the singers in the shows often had to dance a little, or "move well," and the dancers had to be able to carry a tune or sing a little. The dance ensemble numbered about 16 to 20; most shows still had a singing ensemble and a separate dance group but this was soon to change due both to economics and the changing styles of musical comedies. Dance achieved the same importance as the book and the music in musical comedy with Agnes de Mille's choreography for *Oklahoma* (1943). The storyline was never stopped to show off feminine beauties or handsome men in extravagant production numbers for the chorus, as had been done previously. Instead, every dance grew out of the story.

The jazzier music in later musical comedies (see Fig. 1-10) did away with the need for legit or pear-shaped tones in singers. The flat tones of nonsingers or dancers were preferred, and many shows, such as *West Side Story*, had no separate singing ensemble, only dancers who could sing. Choreographers such as Jerome Robbins started to direct the entire production with great success, and *West Side Story* both on stage and in film was generally agreed to be a musical in which the dance became an integral part of the dramatics and in which each performer was expected to be an equally good actor, singer, and dancer. (Earlier films may have had excellent and exciting dancing, such as *Seven Brides for Seven Brothers*, but never dancing as a major element in telling the story and creating

an introduction to jazz dance

FIGURE 1-10 "Your Own Thing," a witty Off-Braodway show that featured many of the well-known rock and disco dances of the 1960s. Copyright © 1968 by National General Music Pub. Co. Copyright © 1968 by Montage Music Pub., Inc. Used by permission of Southwest Amusement Corp., successor in interest by merger to Montage Music.

suspense.) And in 1978, on Broadway, *Dancin'* appeared (choreographed by Bob Fosse), in which the songs and book are secondary to the dancing; in fact, they are almost nonexistent.

THE FUTURE OF JAZZ DANCE

Where do we go from here—new ideas, older concepts, revivals? Who knows! But one thing is sure; dancing, and especially jazz dancing, is here to stay. One reason may be that the audience knows that what they see on a theater or concert stage (a live show) is really what is happening at that instant—it is the choreographer's intent and creativity combined with the dancers' ability and creativity. It has survived the mechanical age. The music and singing, however, are rarely heard exactly as conceived or projected by the singers or musicians in a Broadway show; there may be synching in which the singing is taped, and then the tape is played and synchronized with the staging. The singer-dancer can mouth the words and do a lot of dance movement at the same time, while giving an appearance of singing very well; it is done to varying degrees in stage shows. There usually is amplification, however, and what the audience hears is not what is actually being played or sung at a given instant, but depends on mechanical engineering to balance out the sounds produced, regardless of whether it sounds better from all seats in the house. However, the dancing is happening on stage as seen; a dancer, therefore, must be in top condition for every performance.

Before arriving at today's musical, jazz seemed to go through fad after fad in which one form of dance or another was more prevalent—often also due to the plot—and there was a wide variety: primitive jazz (*Raisin*), Afro-Haitian jazz, Latin jazz, jazz from early social dances (*No, No, Nanette*), rock and roll (*Godspell, Hair*), Hindu jazz (*Alive and Kicking*), balletic jazz (Jerome Robbins), tap jazz (*Pal Joey*), disco jazz (*Dancin'* has some), and musical comedy jazz of a lighthearted variety (*Half a Sixpence*). With *West Side Story,* jazz was back in musical comedy for good in one form or another.

Not everyone has the same idea of what "true jazz" really is, and there is quite a variety of styles. In musical comedies like *Chorus Line* and *Dancin',* several varieties can be found, either separately at times, or all mixed up in what might be called *freeform* jazz (or anything goes in movement) with excellent technique, *plus* a good portion of the basic jazz characteristics. These characteristics, touched on earlier, are: isolations of body parts, involvement of the entire body (use of hips and torso—can a routine be jazz if it does not have any hip isolations?); a going "down into the floor" rather than up into the air (the expression "down into the floor" does not mean that you lie down or sit on the floor, but that the center of gravity is lowered as the knees are bent; the accents of the movement go down with an earthy feeling rather than up—a bluesy jazz number would go down into the floor more than a jazzy ballet with toe shoes); rhythm is part of what jazz dance is all about—syncopation and pauses (a hesitation intensified by channeled but unreleased energy filled with rhythm). There is a greater importance of rhythm than in any other form of dance except, of course, tap dance.

an introduction to jazz dance

As for technique, the demands on a jazz dancer are so great—considering all the areas of dance that can be included in a freeform jazz dance—that many choreographers feel that a dancer must have excellent training in all phases of dance—tap, ballet especially, and, of course, jazz. For someone to go to a disco dance and be able to improvise jazz movements can be lots of fun, but the ability to also do all the forms of jazz dance and learn someone else's choreography requires great skill. As Ann Reinking (star of *Dancin'*) said about dancing Bob Fosse's style: "It requires severe control and extreme freedom. If you go for one and not the other, you're not doing it right."[1]

If you really want to know exactly how "jazzy" a step actually is, things can get complicated. To anyone who has studied only ballet, a *grand emboité devant* from a jazz routine resembles a ballet step. In a jazz class, it could be a descendant of the original shuffling cakewalk, which gradually became a smooth walking step with the body held high (see Fig. 1-11). Then a backward sway was added; then it became the slaves' imitation of a plantation owner; and next it became a prancing strut.[2] With more jump added to it, it looks like a grand emboite devant—right out of centuries-old classical ballet. Remove the turnout, and put in lower prances, and it looks like modern dance prances. So, to someone familiar with ballet, it looks like ballet; to someone familiar with modern, it looks like modern dance; to someone interested in jazz, you have to read more on the origin of jazz to know what it is, and then it depends on what you have read. It also looks much like the cancan, or like one step that belongs in it.

More and more people are being exposed to jazz dance in social dances, in Broadway shows, in the still young jazz concert dance field (Pepsi Bethel's Company and pieces in Alvin Ailey's dance company's repertory), on television ("Dance Fever," "Solid Gold," Channel 13, commercials, and such), and films (*Grease, All That Jazz*). People like jazz dance and want to take classes in it and learn more about it. And that is a good way to do so because jazz dance is a very elusive area, and style, feeling, rhythm, and technique are all important in making it what it is today.

People may go to jazz classes, or try it themselves at home first, for all sorts of reasons, such as:

---

[1]Dunning, Jennifer, "High Stepping into Stardom," *New York Times,* April 2, 1978.

[2]This is not, however, a definitive derivation of the cakewalk. Some believe it originally came from the Seminole Indians in Florida.

It has a contemporary feeling.

They like the beat of the music.

They can do it to a wide variety of music.

It is relaxing and a change of pace after a busy day.

It is refreshing and energizing.

It provides a recreational and social pastime.

It is good for developing coordination.

People can relate to it.

It combines a wide variety of movements; there is something for everybody to enjoy.

It is excellent exercise for every part of the body, and today, when so many people have sedentary jobs and life-styles, exercise with common sense is valuable for everyone, young and old. Jazz dance with its numerous isolation exercises for all parts of the body is excellent therapy.

People want to understand what they see in shows, films, and on TV. Dancing is the thing to do now, and people like to keep up with the trends of the time. Jazz dance is fun to do.

So, read on and have fun dancing!

FIGURE 1-11 *Cake Walk* by Albert Meyers. The American minstrels Williams and Walker in their famous cake-walk. New York, 1890? Watercolor, 22 x 22 in. Collection, The Museum of Modern Art, New York. Given anonymously.

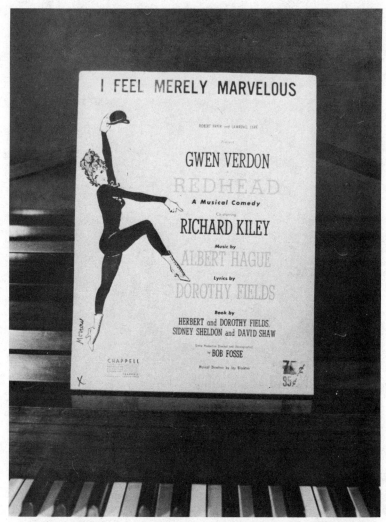

FIGURE 1-12 "I Feel Merely Marvelous," with words and music by Dorothy Fields and Albert Hague, from *Redhead*. Choreographer Bob Fosse created outstanding dances for this show, as well as in *Pippin, Dancin',* and the movie *All That Jazz*. In *Redhead* the blend of Gwen Verdon's superb performance and Bob Fosse's excellent choreography made this show especially memorable. One of the best numbers was the "Pickpocket Tango" with apache dance overtones. Copyright © 1958 by Dorothy Fields and Albert Hague. Chappell & Co., Inc., owner of publication and allied rights throughout the world; international copyright secured. All Rights Reserved. Used by permission.

2
preparation for home practice or class

This chapter includes suggestions concerning suitable attire for class and home practice —comfortable clothes that reveal alignment and body lines, and which allow you to move freely. Some tips on daily practice, muscle tone, good health, diet, and other pertinent areas are also included.

WHAT TO WEAR

Now you're ready to start! Or are you? What have you got on your feet—crepe soles, spike heels, sandals? Those don't sound good— you're not yet a professional doing a show. You must give yourself an advantage, something comfortable that won't stick or slide. That could vary from a pair of jazz shoes (wear rubber soles on slippery floors and leather soles on sticky floors) purchased at a dancewear store—Capezios, Selvas, Herbet's, and others, to bare feet. Some people love dancing in bare feet and feeling the floor beneath their soles; if your feet don't tend to become excessively sticky, even turns are comfy. But it does depend on the floor and on *your* feet, and on the weather—damp or dry. Some beginners find sneakers or bare feet too sticky, so they either find a soft leather, snug, well tied on, almost heelless shoe, such as a specially made jazz shoe with flexible sole, or they wear knobby weave socks. Off come the socks on the lighter, quicker traveling steps across the floor if they feel too slippery, and on they go for the turns if the floor is too sticky.

preparation for home practice or class

Smooth, fine-weave socks or stocking-type footgear are out—too slick. However, to fully exercise your feet, do all the warmup exercises in bare feet, then if you prefer put shoes on for the steps and combinations.

Feet come first because they are what you dance on, but what else to wear? Leotards and tights are a must in some schools, but not necessarily so for jazz, and besides you are practicing at home for a bit. So, choose a comfortable outfit that stays in place well and does not require your attention as you practice. If you are using a mirror (or practicing in a class), your outfit should reveal your body outline and assist you in making and receiving corrections. As you look through your closet, the stores, or television, you will notice a wide variety of outfits, some better suited than others for home or class, for warm, cold, or unexpected weather. If the room is colder than expected, you may wish to add that sweater around your hips and those short leg warmers (or old cut-off sweater sleeves or long woolen socks with the balls of the feet cut off) on your calves. Or you may wish to wear those as well as a leotard with a sleeveless polo shirt on top. After warm-ups, or if the room gets warmer, you can remove the sweater, polo shirt, and calf warmers. They are all lightweight and you are still properly attired with other garments, or you can put them on after warm-ups so your muscles don't get cold. (That old sweater, instead of going around your waistline and hips, can be placed on the floor under those sensitive bones in your back or sides for exercises when you are lying down—instead of complaining and doing nothing constructive about it—or you can bring a small towel.) Certainly any garment coming into contact with your skin—groin and underarm especially—has to be washed each time, which is not necessary for the leg warmers and such, but they remain tighter after being washed. The floor should be clean, but if it isn't spotless, you can wash everything after each practice session or class. The main thing is to make sure that there is nothing on the floor that could be harmful to your bare feet—wash away dirt, or put down a towel during floor exercises.

I prefer having my legs, body, and arms covered, except when practicing at home—there I know how clean the floor is. When I'm elsewhere, I can't tell how clean the floor is until I get there, and then it is too late to change outfits. I also can't tell how warm or cold it will be until I'm there, so I try to be prepared for anything. If you plan to wear a bodysuit for class or home practice, disregard the snaps already there and sew in some hooks and eyes, or wear something else. Substitute elastic straps for the string straps on leotards if you have sloping shoulders. If your tights creep down, buy a longer pair, wear an elastic string around your waistline, and fold the tights over them, or wear an elastic belt and roll the tights over it. Wear a scarf on your head if you do not wish to have your newly washed hair on the floor, or place a towel on the floor. (Better still, wash or damp mop the floor before class!) Hair that is tied back securely will stay off your face as you do head rolls and body bending movements and also make it easier to see your head alignment. Tied-back hair prevents you from looking like an English sheep dog after head movements.

For women, a bra is recommended if you are more than an 'A' cup; it prevents sagging breasts. But no strapless tops, with or without a bra. Your tummy or hips or back may need a little assistance; wear a girdle if you need one until your own muscles form a natural girdle. (We all have a natural girdle, but sometimes we need a little help.) If your skin is sensitive to tight clothes or to moisture from perspiration, wear garments that are porous (as cotton), somewhat loose fitting, and light colors.

Men should wear a supporter for dance and exercise. Slacks, shorts (a decent length and not too tight around the waistline, so you can move), jazz pants, jumpsuits, sweatpants, or heavy tights, and a polo shirt are fine.

For home practice, you might like to have your belly button showing (but *not* in cold weather). This may sound absurd, but when practicing by yourself with a mirror, if you are having any problem aligning your hips while doing upper torso rotations with motion-less hips, or after sitting, carrying bundles, or the like, perhaps improperly, you may find it simple to see that your hips are aligned equally forward by having your belly button facing square front. The same idea holds true for any other area. If your head protrudes, don't wear a turtleneck when practicing at home; if your ankles roll over keep your feet and ankles bare, or wear white socks. You will be able to see yourself more clearly in the mirror. Some people, with or without a mirror, have a wonderful sense of being centered at all times, and they are. They would never need such a suggestion, but if you need it, it may help. This is meant for home practice rather than for the dance class. In class the teacher can always walk around and look at you. There you want a garment that enhances your dancing, but which will not distract you, the other students, or the teacher, or which will focus attention on your clothes rather than on your dance movements.

When you have chosen your outfit, try it on. Bend, twist, reach up, and swing your torso down. Lift your legs to the front, side, and back. Sit with your legs apart. Sit and cross your legs with

preparation for home practice or class

your knees out to the sides. Do a few arm circles and a few situps with bent knees. Stop and look in the mirror—how do you look? If you look O.K., you have a good outfit for class or home practice.

Before starting these exercises, it is assumed that you are in good physical condition and have checked with your doctor about taking on an intensive exercise and dance program if you are not accustomed to regular exercise.

PRACTICAL EXERCISE HINTS

If you really intend to get all you can out of your dance classes or home practice, practice one hour a day. The hour can be split up to suit your schedule. If you don't have time to build up to that amount gradually, here are some hints on how to exercise and use your muscles as a part of your daily activities and with awareness of body positions.

1. Walk daily.

2. Vary the size heels you wear. In this way you stretch the tendons at the back of the heels and give your calves more exercise. Wear comfortable, medium, or low heels while walking.

3. Vary your "carrying arm" and shoulder. That shoulder bag on the left arm tends to cause a ribcage shift to the left side and a hip shift to the right side. Place the shoulder strap on the right shoulder one-half of the time. Carry an infant or the groceries on the right or the left, not constantly on the same side.

4. Men should not carry a wallet always in the same hip pocket. Try the other side.

5. Don't carry heavy groceries if you are tired. Use a carryall; also true for luggage. Don't carry heavy packages just because someone else is able to do so; we are all different. But when you have to pick up something heavy, rest your back and use your thigh muscles by bending your knees.

6. How are you sitting at your home or job? Up tall, evenly on both buttocks, with your straight back resting against the back of a straight chair? Knees in front of your hips? Or are you sprawled out and slumped over, or leaning over on one side? It won't help to prepare your muscles for proper alignment for dancing if you have improper alignment the rest of the day. There is less muscle

imbalance if you use your muscles correctly in a more centered way—the same on both sides of the body—and are aware of what you do. The longer you spend out of shape, the longer it will take you to get into good shape. It also requires a certain amount of mental effort. For some people, a certain amount of home practice of movements they do not have in class is good because it requires more of their concentration than they would put into a previously learned movement. Or perhaps it provides more freedom to think it out for themselves, which, of course, could be done with a movement already learned in class as well. Is your office or home furniture arranged in such a way that you constantly have to twist and turn to the same side to reach for the phone or bookcase or file cabinet? Rearrange the furniture occasionally or do some extra amount of exercise to the other side to compensate. Are you feeling round-shouldered by the end of the day? Get up once in a while; lift your arms overhead and stretch. Rise on the balls of your feet and reach up. Bend down and shake the shoulders out; walk a bit; get a drink of water; reach for something on the top shelf or on the floor. Pull in the tummy tightly; pull up the thighs; tighten the buttocks. Don't let it all hang out.

7. You are tense from stress and overwork. Think of relaxing, and yawn as you stretch or walk. If no one else is in your office, put your feet up on the desk. It's great for relaxing to have the feet higher than your seat. Drop your jaw, shake your shoulders every which way. Lift your right cheek up and down, then the left. Think of having very wide eyes that look out to the sides—right and left both at the same time—as far out to the sides as possible; then look at your nose. Shake your hands out; make a fist; stretch them wide. Press your palms together or sit on your hands with the palms facing down. Is your head jutting forward? Place your palms lightly on the back of your head and press back against them from the base of the head, while relaxing the front part of the neck under the chin so you don't have an army sargeant look or a double chin. Place a medium sized book on the top of your head and feel your spine and neck lengthen as you think of pressing the book up toward the ceiling with your head.

8. Stay within the recommended weight range for your height and bone structure. That is a good weight for your legs to carry so much of the time. You think everything you eat turns to fat? Make a very complete list of what you eat for one week; then eat less than that consistently for two to three months or a year, and see if you don't lose weight. You don't have to talk about it—just do it. Eat

preparation for home practice or class

less than what you usually eat. The food won't taste any better if you eat more of it, so learn to relish a smaller portion and care for yourself, too. Eat a well-balanced meal. If you plan to skip dinner to take a class at that time, eat a snack earlier in the afternoon. Don't dance on a very empty stomach (you need the energy) or on a stuffed stomach. Eat an orange or an apple after practice or class to replenish your energy.

9. Vary your standing and sitting. Don't sit too long at a time; move around a bit. Don't stand for too long at a time; change your position. Walk around or bend your legs and pick something up. If standing, place one foot up on a bench or ledge (it rests the back, too). Change your weight from one leg to the other, not always on the same leg.

10. Sleep and rest; how much sleep is proper depends on the individual. Your muscle tone is better and your energy level, both physical and mental, is higher with proper rest.

11. Do not smoke while doing any kind of physical activity; also be sure to ventilate the room with fresh air occasionally (before or after practice, but preferably not during practice).

All of the above may seem superfluous and not at all relevant, but you will find that the better aligned you are, the more relaxed and fit you are, the more centered (right and left sides more similar), the better equipped you—the instrument—are for dancing.

MUSCLE TONE AND ALIGNMENT

As you look at yourself in the mirror when practicing at home, or as you listen to the teacher if you are taking a class, try to have an objective feeling about corrections and about any present problems you may have. Don't blow them out of proportion. They are there to be improved upon and thought about solely for the sake of finding a solution (and some solutions are very slow and tedious, requiring constant effort and concentration). On the other hand, everyone has some feature that is an asset and that is nice to know. It makes you feel good as you tackle your less desirable features or work on some long-term project. You do want to appreciate your good points and learn what they are.

For dancing, the good points that are basically yours—flexibility, good jumps, sharp turns right on balance, sharp head focus, good posture—are easier to maintain and work on; they are your short-term projects. Those which are not basically yours (maybe you have a tightly knit build and are not flexible; or you are tall and lanky and cannot yet do quick sharp movements) require more constant effort. They are your long-term projects, to be improved on more slowly and carefully. Many of the features that you lack are due to your individual physical build and your individual disposition, so you want to make the most of the good features that you possess as you work toward acquiring others slowly and carefully. Don't overdo it, yet don't do too little. Don't try to achieve flexibility too quickly; it doesn't work that way. There has to be a good amount of strengthening and increased muscle tone along with increased flexibility. When you practice by yourself or in class, be sure that you are aware of what you are doing. Leave the groceries, the office, the children, or whatever out of your thinking during practice time. You should not do the exercises by rote. Keep checking to make sure that you are doing them correctly. Vary the speed, the order, the quantity, and, yes, even the quality—the quality of work should get better.

Did you ever catch sight of yourself in a store window as you walked by? Maybe you were surprised to find yourself looking so tall and erect. Or were you slumping back from the hips, or round-shouldered? What you saw was your alignment. No two people are built precisely the same or align themselves in exactly the same way, but there are a few basic rules. If you are a beginner (and even if you are not), you should not expect your alignment to change overnight. But as you persist in practicing, it will.

Think of a tall, long, relaxed spine reaching up to the top of your head and going on a bit of a diagonal forward so that your weight is over the front half of the feet, but with the heels pressing down into the floor. Lightly lift the heels slightly off the floor and return them to the floor several times to be sure your weight is forward over the balls of the feet.

From the following suggestions aimed at producing proper alignment and muscle tone, try the one that suits you best. A person whose back looks like a "C" can often stand taller and straighter by pulling the waistline back to make the "C" less curved. Those who lean back with hips forward, in front of them, should place both hands together overhead, reach up high and forward as much as possible, and then pull back the whole middle area—waistline, bottom ribs, abdomen—even if they feel as though they are leaning forward a little too much. If you try this, rise up on the balls of the feet in this position and balance; at the same time gradually straighten up just a bit, so you are not leaning forward very much. If you have a side seam on your leotard or polo shirt, this exercise really works. Look at the side view in the mirror and straighten out that seam by adjusting your torso and hips. The straighter you stand, the straighter the seam. You can also think of a line going diagonally forward from your heels to your head; or of lengthening your back and shortening the front area by pulling the front of the hips up toward your ribs. Or, think of an imaginary line pulling up the front of the body and the abdomen, to your waistline, and then transfer that line and continue pulling up through the back of the upper torso and the back of the head; or more simply of a line going diagonally forward from your heels to your head. The abdomen should be pulled in toward the center and up, all the way to your head where it remains as you keep thinking about it and pulling it up. But the ribcage should not be tight, just held up firmly against your spine. You want it to be relaxed enough to breathe freely, so you can expand the back of the torso easily to breathe.

Remember that you can't "let it all hang out"—certainly not all of the time—or that is how you will look. Just look around at yourself and other people as you walk outside; a lot is hanging out— to the front, the back, the sides—and it's not all necessary. You should be able to relax and to pull in. You should be able to pull in that tummy when you want to. You should be able to pull your buttocks up and in when you want to. You should be able to pull your thighs up firmly. When you wish to flop and let go, you should be able to do that also. Let it all hang out and relax—*but not all the time*. That is what you are aiming at as you do your practicing. Think how great you look. This is not a tomorrow project, but a gradual over-the-years project. You won't get there by waiting until tomorrow or the day after that either. Start now and keep going at a regular, disciplined pace until it is a part of your life-style. It takes time and patience. On a day when you have no time, do just a little bit. If you are feeling uptight about something, exercise or napping have been highly recommended; maybe five minutes of exercise, followed by a 10-minute relaxed rest. If you are feeling great, do an extra 15 minutes, or go over some of the steps you especially enjoyed, or that felt challenging to you. You don't have to practice the exercises in the same order each time. If you prefer sitting first, sit. If you prefer isolations standing, then lying down exercises, that is fine, too. You might vary it and see which suits you best. But make sure to do warm-ups and isolations before the steps, because your muscles need the toning up, strength, and flexibility that you gradually acquire from doing these correctly.

SPACE AND DANCE

Space is very basic to dance. You need adequate space for what you are going to do, and it needs to be used well. There should not be a feeling of a traffic jam, either in corners or in the center; it is always a one-way street as you move across the floor if there is more than one person practicing in the room. The floor is cleared of obstructions. If there is a nail jutting out in the flooring, cross two or three bandaids over it; then you won't need one for your foot. In the center, take your space—and that does not mean your neighbor's space; *your* arms and legs do not ever bump into your neighbor's. At home, find a space for yourself where you can swing your arms and legs in every direction without bumping into people or furniture. In class, the teacher sees to it that you have space for the next step and you help by having looked at the layout of furniture and people. Remember that furniture does not move—people do; so once you know the layout of the furniture, it is the spacing of individuals that is important.

The floor should be easy to work on, not slippery, not sticky, and not a surface that makes you feel wiggly like a mat or rug—especially for beginners. It is difficult to either balance or turn on such surfaces.

Don't wear jewelry during dance practice; it gets in the way. If it breaks or falls, you spend half your time looking for it instead of dancing. Chewing is out, too; it's an isolation movement. For jazz dance we try to be aware of one type of isolation movement at a time, and if you are chewing, that is another isolation movement, and you are probably not even aware of it. Besides, you might swallow the gum on head rolls, and you cannot tilt your head as far back while chewing. Naturally, if there is a certain type of movement that you are not supposed to do for medical reasons (perhaps a bad lower back), don't do it. If you are practicing on your own, put aside any exercise that seems not to agree with you for the time being. There are many exercises for the same area, and others might suit you better. Later you can return to the ones you left out, after acquiring more muscle tone and ability. If you feel sore after practicing, a warm bath is always relaxing. Should you feel sore the next day or so, especially at the beginning, do not just give up; a little bit of practice every day will ease away the soreness.

If you have a particular problem you want to work on—say, protruding tummy, poor alignment, or a head that juts forward instead of remaining lined up with your spine, the best way to remedy these and become more aware of them is to find two or three exercises only that you can do just a very little bit at a time, but very often—every single day!

GET SET ...

Now you are ready to begin practice. Read all of the suggestions at the beginning of the chapters and all the notes in the exercises and steps. If you vary any of the steps, arms, or exercises to suit yourself, jot down the changes with stick figures to refresh your memory visually the next time you practice. You don't need a work of art for this purpose; if you cannot draw a straight line, use a ruler. But try to be very aware, as you do them, of exactly how the movement should look and feel, and you will find that not only will your stick figures improve, but you will also be more aware of what you are doing when you dance.

Once you know the steps, put on some records or turn on the radio to practice. You will really enjoy practicing on a regular basis and suddenly acquiring more and more jazz movements that you know and do well. If there is a step you do not understand, leave it out until later; it will probably be clearer then. Add a 10-minute daily workout at a convenient time—when you get up, before going to bed, or to break up your daily routine—and you will progress even more quickly.

Leaf through this book and get an idea of what is coming—all the combinations and routines mention the chapter and number of the steps included in them for easy reference (for example, see Exercise No. 3-2, Chapter 3). Look up the material that is in the Bibliography and add to your background in dance and music. Watch TV shows that feature jazz dance. See Broadway and Off-Broadway shows with jazz dance. Don't forget ticket outlets, such as Duffy's Square at 47th Street and Broadway, in New York City, for half-price tickets on the day of the performance. (London also has them.) Launch into the book. Clear your head of all superfluous thoughts and concentrate on jazz dance. Dance away!

3
*jazz
warm-ups:
exercises*

The exercises in this chapter are for toning up, strengthening, and stretching the muscles. There are some for all parts of the body, and some to be done standing, sitting, and lying down. It is more relaxing if you alternate an exercise done with straight legs with one that is done with bent legs. It is also better—especially for beginners—not to do consecutive exercises using the same muscles. Do an exercise that is primarily for the torso, then one for the legs, or one that does not involve the previously used muscles in exactly the same way. When the muscles are not overtired, they can react more quickly and with more energy.

When you practice, you may want to begin with these warm-up exercises, or you may find that you prefer starting with a few of the standing isolation exercises in Chapter 4, then doing some of these, and then continuing with other isolation exercises in Chapter 4. Everyone should have at his or her command a good repertoire of exercises. It's your body, and the more you become aware of what kind of exercise it needs at any given moment, the better you will feel and the better equipped you will be for dancing.

If you have a weak spot, and you know that you do, such as rolling over the ankles, protruding tummy, or sway back, wear something that makes it obvious—light-colored socks, tights, and leotard. Don't camouflage it with dark garments. You want to see what you do clearly. If you take a class, you want the teacher to be aware of your weak points so he or she can think about them and correct you. You also want to have a very positive attitude about the fact that improvement is always possible with time, patience, and perseverance. If you are a person who gets tense and you hold your breath while practicing, try humming or singing a melody to yourself ("la, la, la" will do fine). As mentioned in the Preface, you will notice that the sketches are mirror images of the text. (Read the text, look at the mirror while trying out steps; you will notice that the mirror image is like the sketch in the book. It faces you and uses its right hand when you use the left.)

jazz warm-ups—standing (number 3-1)

TORSO STRETCHES, BEND, CIRCLE

Stand with feet slightly apart and parallel; arms down at sides. Your body should be centered over both legs, and shoulders even.

COUNTS	MOVEMENT
1–2	Bend forward from the hips to a flat back position with the arms straight forward, alongside your ears. Weight is forward over the front of the foot—with heels on the floor.
3–4	Drop the torso and arms down toward the floor, relaxed, with knees bent, and the weight forward as much as possible.
5–8	Gradually roll up, straightening the spine from the bottom up as the legs straighten, and extend the arms up, then to the sides, still pressing the weight forward.
9–10	Left arm reaches overhead as the torso bends to the right.
11–14	Continue the movement, circling the torso and arms down, relaxed, and over to the left side.
15–16	Straighten up the torso while bringing both arms straight overhead. Pull up the thighs, but do not press the knees back.
17–20	Rise up on the balls of the feet. Pull ankles in toward center as you rise, so they won't sickle, but not on the way down; do not press ankles in toward center or your feet will roll over.
21–22	Heels down; bend the knees. (Watch those ankles; don't roll over.)
23–24	Straighten the legs.
25–96	Repeat 3 times.

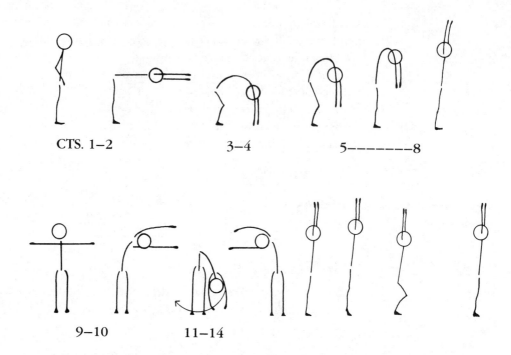

CTS. 1–2   3–4   5–––––––8

9–10   11–14

NOTE: Be sure that the weight is forward over the balls of the feet (with the feet flat [whole foot] on the floor, rather than back on the heels), especially during the torso circling so that you can easily rise up on the balls of the feet on counts 17–20. On counts 3–8 look down and make sure you are centered between your legs, not over one of them. Feet are said to sickle when they adduct—bend in toward the center from the ankles; the toes are closer to the center and the ankles farther away as could happen on counts 17–20.

jazz warm-ups—standing (number 3-2)

<u>BEND FLATBACK, CONTRACT AND RELEASE TORSO, RELAX FORWARD</u>

Stand with feet parallel and hands on groin (where thighs join hips).

COUNTS	MOVEMENT
1–4	Bend torso forward with a flat back and with hands on groin at sides; weight as far forward as possible.
5–6	Contract and round the ribcage backward by pulling in the abdomen, and pressing your waistline and ribs up toward the ceiling while leaving your arms and head where they were.
7–8	Release the whole torso (upper and lower) forward, keeping the weight forward over the front of the feet (with the heels still on the floor).
9–10	Contract the whole torso as in counts 5–6.
11–12	Release the whole torso; elbows will go up slightly.
13–14	Contract the whole torso; elbows will go down slightly.
15–16	Release the whole torso.
17–20	Drop the torso forward, relaxing the neck so that the head drops down (and you can see the back of the room), while bending the legs with the knees over the toes. Drop the arms down toward the floor also.
21–24	Pull abdomen in against your back, roll torso up to stand tall, and rise up on the balls of the feet, and lower the heels while placing hands on groin at sides.

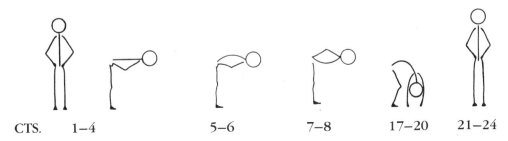

CTS.   1–4   5–6   7–8   17–20   21–24

NOTE: For proper alignment, remember to keep the weight forward over the front of the feet (with the heels on the floor). Pull up the abdomen in front and then think of that imaginary line, pulling up, being transferred to the back of your upper torso and the back of your head. You will find that you have good balance up on your toes in this position, as well as a nice flat tummy and a long straight back. Do the exercise in a relaxed, easy manner the first few times, then gradually bring the weight more forward and straighten the back more on the flat back.

jazz warm-ups—sitting
(number 3-3)

LONG-SITTING POSITION:
STRETCHES FOR FEET, ARM PRESSES

Sit with legs straight in front of you, long spine, and hands on knees.

COUNTS	MOVEMENT
1–2	Stretch the ankles and point the toes down.
3–4	Flex the feet and press the toes up toward the calf.
5–16	Repeat 3 times.
17–20	Circle the feet to the right, making sure the knees do not move.
21–32	Repeat 3 times.
33–64	Reverse to other side.
65–66	Flex the feet and curl the toes at the same time.
67–68	Keep the feet flexed and stretch the toes apart, wide.
69–80	Repeat 3 times counts 65-68.

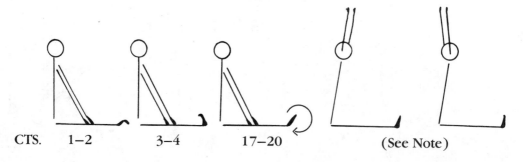

CTS.   1–2   3–4   17–20   (See Note)

NOTE: If you have the kind of knees that press into the floor, causing the heels to be off the floor when you flex your feet (and it is not just heavy calves that cause this), relax the knees slightly and leave the heels on the floor so you do not continuously press the knees back. Shake legs out in front to relax them.

For slumpers (during the foot exercises), follow with this: Sit well forward over your hips, arms straight overhead, press arms back 8 times. If your feet get cramps, wiggle your toes; do feet exercises more regularly, a little bit at a time.

jazz warm-ups: exercises

jazz warm-ups—sitting (number 3-4)

TORSO STRETCH, ARM OVERHEAD, CROSS LEGGED

Sit with legs crossed, knees out at sides, both feet on the floor, two hands on the floor at sides, and long spine. Left leg front.

COUNTS	MOVEMENT
1–2	Lift left arm overhead, keeping the elbow back. Bend torso to the right, being sure to leave the buttocks on the floor. Head looks up at ceiling. Right elbow bends slightly, if necessary, to be sure the shoulder is held down.
3–4	Straighten torso, open the arm side, and return it to the floor.
5–8	Reverse counts 1–4.
9–32	Repeat 3 times.
33–40	Shake the legs out straight in front by bending them slightly and straightening them several times. Cross them again with the right leg front.
41–80	Reverse counts 1-40.

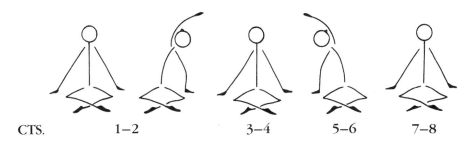

CTS.	1–2	3–4	5–6	7–8

NOTE: Keep the shoulders back, elbow back, and head up. Be sure to press the hips and buttocks down into the floor as you bend sideways.

jazz warm-ups—sitting (number 3-5)

TORSO PULSES, FORWARD, SITTING

Sit with legs straight front (long sitting position); arms forward with jazz hands (hands stretched wide with palms facing each other; see No. 5-3, Chapter 5).

COUNTS	MOVEMENT
1–8	Pulse (small bouncing movement) forward 8 times from hips with arms extended forward and jazz hands, toes pointed. These are small pulses.
9–12	Arms overhead as you sit up tall.
13–16	Flex feet and extend arms forward with jazz hands.
17–32	Repeat with flexed feet.

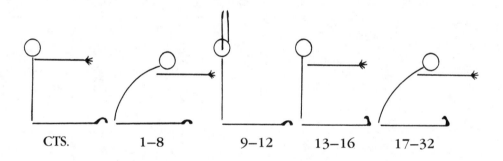

| CTS. | 1–8 | 9–12 | 13–16 | 17–32 |

NOTE: If your knees are pressing into the floor and your heels are off the floor, relax the knees slightly and leave the heels on the floor, so your knees will not be continuously pressing backward. (If you have heavy calves and that is what causes your heels to be off the floor, it is unimportant.) *Shake legs out* by rapidly flexing and straightening legs, alternately, on the floor to relax them.

jazz warm-ups—sitting (number 3-6)

KNEEOVERS

Sit with knees bent and pointing straight up (hook sitting position); hands on the floor in back of you.

COUNTS	MOVEMENT
1–2	Roll knees over toward the floor on the right side, leaving the feet one on top of the other, with the right foot on the floor. Upper torso is straight and faces front.
3–4	Return to center position and pull abdomen in against your back.
5–8	Reverse.
9–16	Repeat counts 1-8.

CTS. 1–2 3–4 5–6

NOTE: This is a good relaxer for the legs and hips, after a straight-legged exercise like No. 3-5. Any bent-legged exercise would be relaxing, but this one is also good for the hips. See Index for specific pages with notes on relaxing.

jazz warm-ups—sitting
(number 3-7)

HALF SITDOWNS

Sit with legs bent, feet flat on the floor and knees pointing up toward the ceiling (hook sitting position). Hands under the legs, holding thighs.

COUNTS	MOVEMENT
1–4	Round the back, tuck the hips under, leave the shoulders forward, and tuck the head down. Roll down one vertebrae after another, pulling in the abdomen firmly against your back and continuously tucking the hips under until your waistline reaches the floor and no further. Feet remain flat on the floor.
5–8	Slowly roll up to tall sitting while pulling in the abdomen.
9–32	Repeat 3 times.
33–64	Repeat 4 times, but with the arms extended out in front instead of holding the thighs.

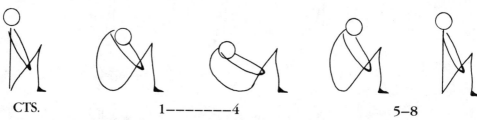

CTS.   1--------4   5–8

NOTE: If these sitdowns are difficult for you to do, imagine that your feet are very heavy and press your legs and feet forward into the floor as you roll down. If you tend to sit very tall, think of slumping as you start to roll down to your waistline in order to round your back.

OPPOSITIONAL STRETCH STRIDE SITTING, HIP STRETCH

Sit with legs apart and straight; feet flexed. Rotate the legs, inwardly if necessary, so that the flexed feet point straight up to the ceiling, not to the back of the room, and the knees also point straight up and not to the back of the room. The muscles on both sides of the legs are used more correctly in this manner. Arms are extended out to the sides.

COUNTS	MOVEMENT
	Torso reaches forward as low as possible with the arms rounded in front. Be aware of your buttocks and thighs on the floor so that you do not lift them off the floor on the next counts.
1–2	Twist the torso to the right and touch the right leg, as close to the foot as possible, with the left hand. The right arm goes to the back. The buttocks and thighs remain exactly as they were before—on the floor.
3–4	Then torso and arms reach forward in front.
5–8	Reverse to the other side.
9–16	Repeat counts 1-8.
17–20	Sit up tall with arms coming overhead and opening out to the sides, and point the toes.
21–36	Repeat counts 1-20, but with the toes pointed.

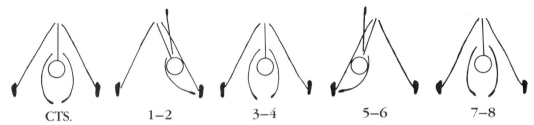

CTS.	1–2	3–4	5–6	7–8

NOTE: Do not lift the thighs or buttocks off the floor in your enthusiasm to get your hand to touch your toes; just touch your knee or calf at first.

To relax your legs or groin leave the feet together on the floor in front and lift hips up, either with straight or bent knees, abdomen in. If you stretch up very high, be sure to press your arms into your sockets as you do this.

jazz warm-ups—lying down (number 3-9)

FRONT LEG RAISES (ON BACK)

On your back with legs together and toes pointing, abdomen pulls up toward your head. Waistline presses down toward the floor, arms extend side like a T-bar, with palms facing up.

COUNTS	MOVEMENT
1–2	Pull up muscles of the right thigh, then lift your straight right leg up as high as possible, with other leg remaining on the floor, straight, and with shoulders relaxed down on the floor.
3–4	Lower right leg to the floor, keeping the legs straight and the abdomen pulled up. Waistline remains on the floor, if possible, or as close to the floor as your body build allows.
5–8	Reverse to the left.
9–64	Repeat 7 times.

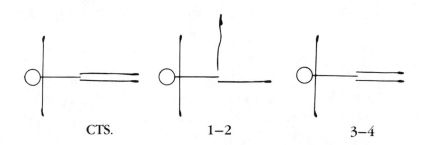

CTS.   1–2   3–4

NOTE: Remember to use your feet as directed in all these warm-ups. If you can train your feet to point fully or flex fully when the lying down exercises require you to do so, they will more readily point or flex, as desired, when you do the dance steps standing up.

Breathe in as you raise the leg and breathe out as you lower the leg, since this is the point at which it is most difficult to pull up the abdomen, and so it is preferable to have less air inside yourself. Shake legs out along the floor—alternately flex and straighten legs—to relax legs.

jazz warm-ups—lying down (number 3-10)

KNEEOVERS (ON BACK)

Knees bent and pointing up to the ceiling (hook lying position). Arms at the sides like a T-bar with palms up, or hands under your head with elbows down on the floor.

COUNTS	MOVEMENT
1–4	Bring the knees over to the right side on or toward the floor, with the side of the right foot remaining on the floor and with left foot over the right foot. Relax the hips and thighs and pull the abdomen in against the back. Head looks to the left at the flat shoulder staying on the floor, as the knees go to the right.
5–8	Return knees to center as at the beginning. At the same time, flatten the entire back on the floor with the tummy pulling in flat.
9–16	Reverse—kneeovers to the left and look right.
17–64	Repeat 3 times.

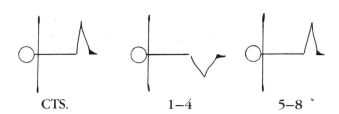

CTS.   1–4   5–8

NOTE: The shoulders remain flat on the floor throughout. *Relax them down.* This is a good exercise for relaxing legs after No. 3-9, front leg raises.

jazz warm-ups—lying down (number 3-11)

HEAD RAISES (ON BACK)

On your back with legs together and toes pointing, arms extended at sides like a T-bar, with palms facing up. Shoulders relax down or press down on the floor; abdomen pulls up and waistline presses down toward floor.

COUNTS	MOVEMENT
1–4	Raise head up, leaving shoulders flat on the floor and abdomen pulled up.
5–8	Relax head down.
9–12	Leave the back of the head on the floor, but raise the chin up so you can see the back of the room; shoulders down.
13–16	Relax.
17–64	Repeat 3 times.

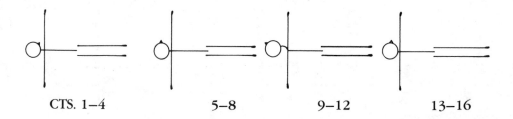

CTS. 1–4   5–8   9–12   13–16

NOTE: Shoulders remain down on the floor throughout. This is a good exercise for the shoulders and neck. It is also excellent for the tummy, if you pull it up, and every time you lift your head you can see if you have done so! Remember, if it is flat when you are lying on your back, you should be able to hold it flat when standing, with a little effort.

jazz warm-ups—lying down
(number 3-12)

TURNED-OUT KNEE BOUNCES, EXTENSION (ON SIDE)

On your side with both knees bent; one arm is under your head either straight or bent, and the other is in front of you on the floor to assist you in maintaining your position and balance.

COUNTS	MOVEMENT
1–4	Turn out top leg and lift the bent knee; pulse it in toward chest or shoulder 4 times with the foot pointed. (Remember that a pulse is a small bouncing movement.)
5–6	Extend the leg straight up from the knee with the toes pointed. (It will be somewhere between front and side, depending on your build.)
7–8	Flex the foot.
9–12	Lower the straight leg down to the floor with the foot flexed.
13–16	Bend the knee and relax the leg over the other leg.
17–64	Repeat 3 times and then turn over to the other side.
65–128	Reverse.

CTS. 1–4 5–6 7–8

9–12 13–16

NOTE: Start the exercise easily with less turnout and extending the leg lower down, and gradually try to increase the turnout and extend the leg up higher. Be sure to relax completely as you bend the leg down over the other leg at the end of the exercise.

jazz warm-ups—lying down
(number 3-13)

ARCH TORSO, HALF SITUP

On your back with knees bent facing the ceiling (hook lying position). Arms are extended to the sides (T-bar), shoulder height, with palms up or behind your head.

COUNTS	MOVEMENT
1–2	Arch the upper and lower torso. Keep the head, arms, and shoulders on the floor. Press the top of the pelvis forward and the bottom of the pelvis back, pressing your seat into the floor and relaxing the small of the back. The head, arms, and shoulders move down slightly toward the hips, on the floor as you arch your torso. Elbows remain on the floor.
3–4	Flatten the back on the floor.
5–6	Pull the abdomen in firmly and flatten it as you raise the head, arms, and shoulders up in front, and lift the upper torso to your waistline only. Hands remain in back of your head as you come up.
7–8	Relax the torso, head, shoulders, and arms down into the floor.
9–32	Repeat 3 times.

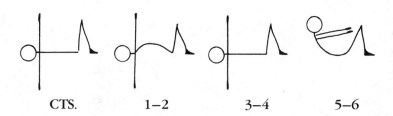

| CTS. | 1–2 | 3–4 | 5–6 |

NOTE: If you relax the shoulders and arms down on the floor during all the floor exercises, you automatically get a passive exercise and stretch your back and shoulders flat, without having to use much energy to do so. Be sure to press your seat into the floor and relax the small of the back as you arch the torso. It is relaxing for the small of the back. This exercise can also be done with straight legs; the toes point as the torso arches and the feet flex when the upper torso (to the waistline only) lifts off the floor.

jazz warm-ups—lying down (number 3-14)

SIDE LEG RAISES

> Start on left side with left elbow on floor under the left shoulder, and the lower arm and hand pointing in front of you. Right arm reaches up diagonally to the side. The bottom leg is bent, the top one is straight. The ribcage is pulled up so the weight is not sinking into the left shoulder.

COUNTS	MOVEMENT
1–2	Raise straight right leg up to the side (or slightly front of side) with the leg turned out, toes pointed, thighs pulled up, and knees straight. As you raise the leg, be sure to pull up through the ribcage, so it is not rounding down at the side toward the floor.
3–4	Lower the leg to the floor.
5–16	Repeat 3 times.
17–20	Roll over on your back and shake your legs out along the floor.
21–24	Roll over to the other side and be ready, in starting position to reverse the exercise.
25–44	Reverse counts 1-20.

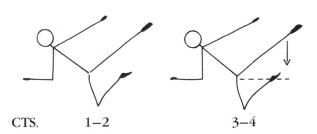

CTS.   1–2   3–4

> NOTE: Do not slump through the ribcage, but pull up the ribcage so that both sides are the same length. The raised leg may be turned out or not, as you wish. If you turn it out, be sure to raise it, not directly to the side, but somewhat in front of side, especially if you tend to extend the leg incorrectly with the knee bent, or if your thigh gets sore. (It should not be sore.) Be sure not to lift the leg up very high at first.

jazz warm-ups—lying down
(number 3–15)

RAISE UPPER TORSO, PULL IN ABDOMEN

On abdomen, feet together, chin on floor, hands behind back.

COUNTS	MOVEMENT
1–4	Pull in abdomen and raise torso up, lifting head up toward ceiling.
5–8	Lower torso to floor and relax.
9–12	Lift abdomen off the floor, leaving the chin and hips on the floor.
13–16	Relax.
17–20	Hands on back; pull in abdomen and lift up torso and head.
21–24	Lower torso to floor and relax.
25–28	Lift abdomen up off the floor, leaving chin, hips, feet on the floor. (This is not difficult, you should not look as if you are working too hard.)
29–32	Relax.
33–128	Repeat 3 times counts 1–32.

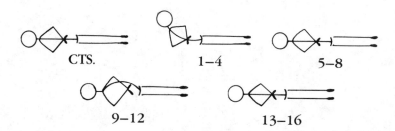

NOTE: The feet remain on the floor throughout. Counts 25–32 are a very simple exercise that is excellent for the lower back, following the torso raises. Just be sure not to try to make too much out of this exercise; easy does it, chin and hips stay down. Be sure to wipe away any dust that is on the floor in front of your face; there is a tendency to inhale as you lift up the torso, and you will inhale the dust if it is there.

FLUTTER KICKS (BACK), PULL IN ABDOMEN

On abdomen, chin resting on hands, feet close together.

COUNTS	MOVEMENT
1	Lift the left straight leg off the floor about 2 inches (think of lifting the thigh, not the foot).
2	Lower the left straight leg, at the same time raising the right straight leg.
3	Lower the right straight leg, at the same time raising the left straight leg.
4–12	Continue doing the flutter kicks as above with torso relaxed, shoulders relaxed, and abdomen pulled up. Thighs come off the floor slightly as the leg lifts up; the knees are straight.
13–16	Pull abdomen in off the floor, leaving everything else as is.
17–20	Relax the abdomen.
21–40	Repeat.

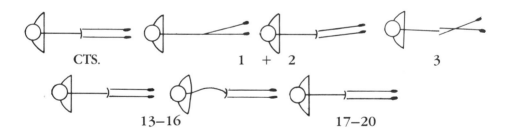

CTS.   1 + 2   3

13–16   17–20

NOTE: Be sure that thighs are pulled up and legs are straight.

jazz warm-ups—on hands and knees (number 3–17)

STRAIGHTEN LEGS, WALK HANDS TO FEET, STAND

Start with hands under the shoulders, on the floor; knees on the floor under the hips; balls of the feet on the floor (that is the part of the toes that you stand on, not the top, but the bottom).

COUNTS	MOVEMENT
1–4	Straighten the legs with the balls of the feet on the floor, head as far down as possible, and hands on the floor.
5–12	Take 8 counts to walk the hands back toward the feet. If you can not usually place your fingertips on the floor when you bend forward with straight legs, you will have to bend the knees to finish walking your hands to your feet.
13–20	Do 8 small pulses (small bouncing movements) with the whole torso and arms down toward your feet; straight legs if possible. People with hyperextended knees (that sway or curve toward the back when the feet are parallel) would do well to pull the thighs up, but to relax the knees slightly so as eventually to diminish rather than to increase this curve. Legs will look straight.
21–24	Fingertips on the floor while relaxing the torso and the back of the hips and thighs.
25–28	Knuckles on the floor, if they reach there. (Otherwise, just relax while the torso is bent over.)
29–32	Palms of hands on the floor; bend the elbows and touch your forehead to your knees, if you can (or relax down).
33–40	Slowly roll the torso up, starting from the base of the spine and finishing with the head, until you are standing tall.

CTS.   1–4   5———————12   13–32   33–40

4

jazz warm-ups: isolations

Isolations are a very important characteristic of jazz dance. These isolation exercises are meant to develop the ability to move various sections of the body—either in isolation or in conjunction with other parts of the body—with ease.

For a beginners' class especially, it is a good idea to alternate the use of the various parts of the body to avoid overtiring the muscles. It is also a good idea to alternate bent leg exercises with straight leg ones. Exercises using ribcage and hip twist, rotations, and shifts (moving a part of the body directly back, side, or front without tilting) should be alternated with some centered ones, such as the head peck or bending and straightening of the legs (where both sides of the body are the same). With that in mind, in this section the isolations for any one part of the body are not placed together, but in what should be a comfortable order for the beginner.

Start by doing smaller isolation movements at first; as you become better at isolating various parts of the body, try doing larger movements, but return to the smaller ones occasionally for a more completely isolated movement. If you start with larger movements, there is a tendency to move other parts of the body as well—this is what we wish to avoid. Enjoy doing these exercises. Start by doing a few, then alternate them with the warm-ups from Chapter 3, sitting and lying down, and add a few more isolations. Practice these until you know them; then begin to add new ones and eliminate the ones you already know if you have a limited amount of practice time. But go slowly at first and concentrate on what you are doing. All the isolations in this chapter are used in the steps and combinations that follow in later chapters. As mentioned before, the sketches are mirror images of the text; they face you and move to their left as you move to your right, much as your mirror image in the mirror does. The photographs are a quiz. Can you identify the steps shown in them?

jazz warm-ups—isolations (number 4–1)

BODY STRETCH WITH HIP ISOLATION

Stand with feet apart and parallel, arms overhead.

COUNTS	MOVEMENT
1–2	Bend right knee, press right hip out to the side. Press right palm straight up toward ceiling with wrist sharply flexed. Be sure the feet are facing front, without any turnout, and the right knee is bent directly over the right foot. Press into the floor, and at the same time press up to the ceiling to get a stretch throughout the whole body (See No. 5–4, Chapter 5).
3–4	Reverse to the left.
5–8	Repeat right and left.
9–10	Straighten both legs; arms are extended out at sides. Bend forward from the hips with torso parallel to floor—flat back.
11–12	Drop torso down, relaxed, with head and arms hanging down and neck relaxed. Fingertips are close to the floor.
13–16	Slowly unroll torso upward starting from pelvis and finishing with the head. Arms hang down from the shoulders. Abdomen is pulled up against your back.
17–64	Repeat entire exercise 3 times.

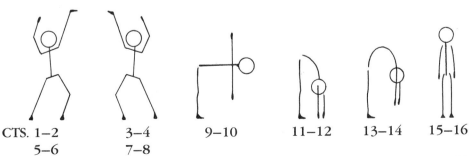

CTS. 1–2   3–4   9–10   11–12   13–14   15–16
     5–6   7–8

NOTE: On counts 11–12 and 13–15, be sure to relax the neck, as though you wanted to see the back of the room. You can see it on counts 11–12.

As you look at the sketches, realize that they are mirror images of the text. The text says "right palm overhead," but the mirror–imaged sketch shows the left palm overhead.

jazz warm-ups—isolations (number 4–2)

HEAD SHIFT (FRONT AND BACK)

Stand with feet slightly apart and parallel, with arms down at sides.

COUNTS	MOVEMENT
1	Shift (move directly without bending) the head forward without moving the shoulders.
2	Return the head to center.
3	Shift the head backward without moving the shoulders.
4	Return the head to center.
5–16	Repeat 3 times.

CTS.   1   2   3   4

NOTE: On count 1, be sure *not* to move the whole torso forward along with the head. Try very small head movements at first.

Advanced beginners can try these head movements while maintaining a good jazz hand position with the arms extended at the sides, (see No. 5–3, Chapter 5), or with flat hands on groin front.

Pecking is a movement derived from animal imitations— the chicken—and can be found in the Yanvallou dance of Trinidad and a Dahomean dance of West Africa, among others.

jazz warm-ups—isolations
(number 4–3)

SHOULDERS UP AND DOWN

Stand with feet slightly apart and parallel, with arms down at sides.

COUNTS	MOVEMENT
1–2	Lift both shoulders.
3–4	Lower both shoulders.
5–16	Repeat 3 times.

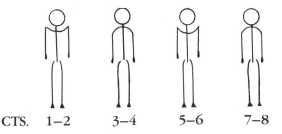

CTS.   1–2   3–4   5–6   7–8

SHOULDERS—FORWARD, BACK

Stand with feet slightly apart and parallel, arms either down or extended out at sides.

COUNTS	MOVEMENT
1	Lift right shoulder.
2	Bring right shoulder down in front.
3	Lift right shoulder.
4	Lower right shoulder back in place.
5–8	Reverse—left.
9–32	Repeat 3 times.

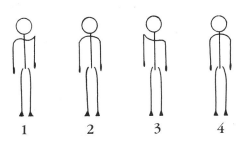

1   2   3   4

jazz warm-ups—isolations (number 4–4)

HIP TWIST

Stand with feet together, parallel, knees bent, and heels slightly off the floor; arms extended at sides.

COUNTS	MOVEMENT
1–2	Pivot on the balls of both feet, twisting the hips, knees and legs to the right, while the upper torso remains facing front as much as possible. The arms do not move.
3–4	Return hips and legs to original position.
5–8	Reverse to the left.
9–32	Repeat 3 times.

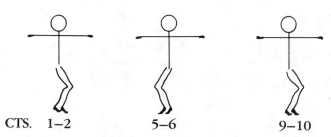

CTS.   1–2   5–6   9–10

NOTE: Try to isolate lower torso and limbs from upper torso as much as possible. Try doing smaller movements if your shoulders or upper torso do not remain motionless.

The "twist" originally dates back to early Afro–American dances. It reappeared and caught on all over America in 1960; its popularity was largely due to Chubby Checkers and New York City's Peppermint Lounge, where the "jet set" twisted. Endless variations appeared—either with one or both feet on the floor and the other raised to the side, front or back. A twisting action from the hips through the feet was taught and described as drying your backside with a large towel. Excellent exercise and lots of fun was the general conclusion.

RIBCAGE SHIFT SIDE

Stand with feet parallel and slightly apart; arms are extended at sides.

COUNTS	MOVEMENT
1–2	Pull up the abdomen and lift the ribcage directly over to the right side without bending; in other words, shift.
3–4	Return to center and relax (abdomen does not relax).
5–6	Pull up the abdomen and shift the ribcage over to the left side.
7–8	Return to center and relax; abdomen is still pulled up.
9–32	Repeat 3 times.

CTS.   1–2   3–4   5–6   7–8

NOTE: Be sure to lift the bottom ribs and shift the entire ribcage evenly to the side, not just the top ribs. The whole upper torso including the head shifts to the side. Keep the shoulder line parallel to the floor. Do not tilt the ribcage. If you find this difficult, place arms out to the sides and think of touching the wall at the right, then at the left, at a spot slightly higher than shoulder height, and see if this helps you to isolate the ribcage more easily. If you are practicing without a mirror, try to become aware of keeping the shoulders parallel to the floor when shifting the ribcage by placing fingers on collarbones on either side. *Bend* to the right and to the left; notice how it feels. Then *shift* the ribcage right and left with fingers remaining on collarbones and be aware of the shoulders moving straight across. Notice the difference when bending and shifting. Now practice it as written with the counts. If it is difficult for you to isolate your ribs in this side shift, try the forward and back ribcage shift (No. 4–11) first. It may be easier for you.

jazz warm-ups—isolations
(number 4–6)

SHOULDERS FORWARD AND BACK (SHIMMY)

Stand with feet apart and parallel. Drop the torso, head, and arms forward from the pelvis, relaxed.

COUNTS   MOVEMENT

1–4   While you are bent forward, shake the shoulders up and down alternately. The hips and thighs remain motionless; as the torso comes up gradually, the shoulders will shake forward and back.

5–8   Continue shaking the shoulders forward and backward while raising the torso with the arms extended in front of the shoulders.

9–10   Continue shaking the shoulders with the arms extended in front; bend back and arch the upper torso slightly from the waistline.

11–12   Continue shaking the shoulders and return the torso to center position over the hips.

13–16   Continue shaking the shoulders and lower the torso, head, and arms to the original starting position.

17–64   Repeat 3 times.

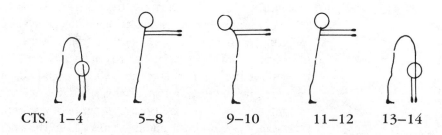

CTS.   1–4   5–8   9–10   11–12   13–14

NOTE: On counts 1–4, it is very easy to keep the hips motionless. If you concentrate on pressing the hips and thighs down into the floor and continuing to keep them motionless as you raise the torso and bend back, you will find it much easier to do so, while shaking just the shoulders.

Photo by Clotilde

jazz warm-ups—isolations (number 4–7)

<u>HIP LIFT SIDE</u>

Stand with feet apart and parallel; knees bent over toes; arms extended at sides.

COUNTS	MOVEMENT
1–2	Lift hips up to the right, with both knees still bent and without moving the ribcage.
3–4	Return to center.
5–6	Lift hips up to the left side.
7–8	Return to center.
9–32	Repeat 3 times.

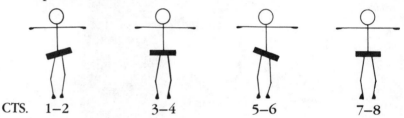

CTS.   1–2   3–4   5–6   7–8

<u>For Advanced Beginners</u>

Syncopated counts are as follows, with an accent on a sharp hip lift side.

+a	Hips are centered.
1	Move the hip and lift it sharply to the right, with the accent on count 1. Be sure to reach up and to the right with the upper torso, so it does not tilt down toward the right hip. (In other words, delay starting the movement, but then rush and get there *on the beat* for that hip lift side.
2	Return hips to center.
+a3–4	Reverse to the left.

NOTE: The abdomen is pulled up throughout, the knees remain bent, and the ribcage remains still. Try smaller movements of the hips if your ribcage moves. Heels remain on the floor.

Jazz steps derived from Latin dances often have hip lifts to the side.

jazz warm-ups—isolations (number 4–8)

<u>LEG PLIÉ (BEND) AND RELEVÉ (RISE)</u>

Stand with feet slightly apart and parallel, arms down.

COUNTS	MOVEMENT
1–2	Bend the knees slowly, keeping the heels on the floor. Be sure not to roll over on the inner border of the feet. Keep the knees over the toes, and be sure that all the toes, especially the little toe and the knuckle of the big toe, remain on the floor.
3–4	Slowly straighten the legs.
5–6	Slowly rise on the balls of the feet. Press the ankles in toward the center, if they tend to roll out at the sides. Concentrate on this before rising on the balls of the feet; afterward it is too late.
7–8	Slowly lower the heels to the floor.
9–32	Repeat 3 times.

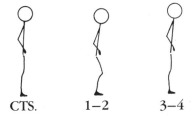

CTS.   1–2   3–4

NOTE: Keep the weight forward over the front of the feet. Abdomen pulls up; the front, top of the hips pull up toward the bottom of the ribs. The waistline presses back, thus lengthening the back of the whole torso (upper and lower) without getting an undesired tucked-under look through the hips (which also makes the front of the thighs look undesirably thicker). On counts 5–8, do not rise up high on the balls of the feet to start with. After several months' practice you may gradually rise up higher as you acquire flexibility and strength. This exercise, with a turnout of the legs, has been done for 250 years during ballet classes as a part of the barre exercises in the five positions of the feet. It was adapted for use by jazz classes because it is an excellent exercise for the calves and the tendons in the back of the heels. It is used for modern dance also, often without a turnout.

LEG EXTENSIONS (DÉVELOPPÉ)

Stand with feet slightly apart and parallel; arms extended at sides.

COUNTS	MOVEMENT
1–2	Lift the right foot up next to the left leg with the toes pointing.
3–4	Extend the right leg out to the front with the toes pointed.
5–6	Flex the foot with the leg still extended to the front.
7–8	Lower the right leg in place.
9–16	Repeat counts 1–8 with right leg front.
17–32	Reverse counts 1–8 with left leg 2 times front.
33–36	Turn both feet out slightly (as you turn out both legs).
37–76	Repeat counts 1–32 (same pattern—2 times with right leg and 2 times with left leg), not front but diagonally side, or a direction between front and true side; this permits you to keep hips facing front and to keep hips parallel to the floor during extensions.
77–152	Repeat with higher extensions. The hips are parallel to the floor. Standing leg pulls up; the working leg presses in at the groin (where hips and thigh meet at the side); the knee pulls up. Maintain all this and try to extend the leg as high as the knee was previously raised on counts 1–2.

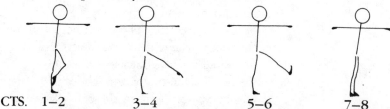

CTS.   1–2   3–4   5–6   7–8

NOTE: Start with low extensions, being careful to keep the hips parallel to the floor. Pull up on the standing hip, keeping that leg straight. Press the working leg in toward yourself where the thigh and hip join, especially on diagonal side extensions to help keep the hips at the same level and over the standing leg. The hips should be evenly centered over the standing foot. Shoulder line remains over or in front of the hip line, so the torso does not lean back.

Anyone who has studied ballet will recognize this isolation exercise as a développé devant, followed by a développé à la seconde (to the side). We see the addition of the modern dance influence of doing ballet-type exercises with flexed feet and no turnout (which evolved in modern dance when it was finally recognized that perhaps ballet did have a few good points, after going through a stage when ballet was completely out). All this was included in jazz dance warm-ups, with the addition of doing the foot flexing as an isolation movement before lowering the leg.

jazz warm-ups—isolations (number 4–10)

KNEE ROLL

Start with the feet slightly apart and parallel, knees bent, arms extended out to the sides, feet flat on the floor.

COUNTS	MOVEMENT
1	Press the knees and hips out toward the left side.
+	Roll the knees and hips toward the front, lifting the heels slightly off the floor and pressing the hips forward also. The level of the upper torso and head stays the same throughout the knee roll. It does not go up or down.
a	Knees and hips go to the right side and heels return to the floor with bent knees.
2	Pause.
3–8	Repeat 3 times.
9–12	Rise on balls of feet with arms overhead and stretch the legs and hips up, just to relax.
13–24	Reverse.

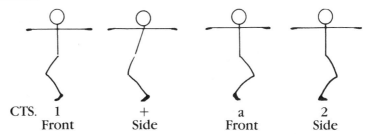

CTS.   1   +   a   2
Front   Side   Front   Side

NOTE: Try to move the upper torso as little as possible during the knee roll; no up-and-down movements of the torso or head should be made.

73

jazz warm-ups—isolations
(number 4–11)

RIBCAGE SHIFT, FRONT AND BACK

Stand with feet slightly apart and parallel; arms either out at sides, or on abdomen or hips.

COUNTS	MOVEMENT
1–2	Pull in the abdomen, lift up the ribcage, and shift it forward.
3–4	Return to center.
5–6	Shift the ribcage back. The body weight, as usual, is held forward over the front half of the feet.
7–8	Return to center.
9–32	Repeat 3 times.

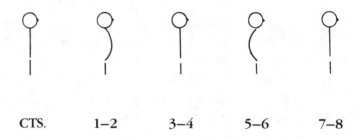

| CTS. | 1–2 | 3–4 | 5–6 | 7–8 |

NOTE: Be sure the abdomen is pulled in throughout. Only the ribcage shifts forward, not the tummy. Keep weight forward. If you have trouble with the side shifts of the ribcage (No. 4–5), try this forward and back shift first; it often helps. If you find the shift to the back difficult, make believe you are slumping while carrying a lot of books in front of your chest. For the forward shift of the ribcage, think of your chest reaching forward, like a chicken, with the wings back and breastbone forward (just out of the freezer about to be roasted).

jazz warm-ups—isolations *(number 4–12)*

HIP ROTATIONS

Stand with feet slightly apart, under the hips, and parallel; hands on collarbone on either side, or down at sides.

COUNTS	MOVEMENT
	Without moving the shoulder area at all, rotate the hips in a counterclockwise direction while legs remain straight. Make very small movements at the beginning to be sure to isolate the hip area. Pull the spine very tall and relaxed, and make 1½ smooth circles.
1	Hips to right side. (This will be a counterclockwise circle.)
2	Hips front.
3	Hips to left side.
4	Hips back.
5	Hips to right side.
6	Hips front.
7	Hips to left side.
8	Hips center.
9–16	Reverse in clockwise direction.

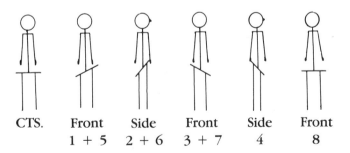

CTS.	Front	Side	Front	Side	Front
	1 + 5	2 + 6	3 + 7	4	8

NOTE: If you are working without a mirror, be aware of the shoulder area staying very still under your fingers at the collarbones; then extend arms out at sides.

Rotation of the pelvis, usually with bent knees, is an Afro-American movement found in American social dances around 1913, such as "ballin' the jack" (a hit dance in the *Ziegfeld Follies*; it became popular as a result of this show). It is also found in the "kootchy-ma-cooch," likewise known as the "congo grind." (A grind is a hip rotation.) Such dances were prevalent in the tenderloin districts (the "shady" side of town) in the west, or the levee areas in the south, and then swept the east, from 1913 to 1930. These hip movements, commonly known as bumps and gri..ds (bumps are hip lifts), were also found in burlesque shows and are seen in modern revivals of burlesque-type shows, such as the Broadway hit of 1980, *Sugar Babies*.

jazz warm-ups—isolations (number 4–13)

HEAD ROLL

Stand with feet slightly apart and parallel, and arms down at sides.

COUNTS	MOVEMENT
1–2	Drop head down in front. Think short, wide neck to relax.
3–4	Roll head to right, so right ear is over right shoulder.
5–6	Roll head to back. Shoulders remain still.
7–8	Roll head over to the left shoulder.
9–32	Repeat 3 times.
33–64	Reverse to left. Drop the jaw slightly to relax.

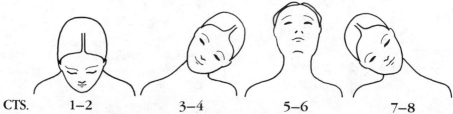

| CTS. | 1–2 | 3–4 | 5–6 | 7–8 |

NOTE: If your neck gets tight on head rolls, keep your head in closer to you, as though you were trying to shorten your neck, rather than stretching it out long. Be sure to keep shoulders still. To relax the neck during head rolls, drop the jaw slightly.

jazz warm-ups: isolations

jazz warm-ups—isolations (number 4–14)

<u>LEG TURN IN</u>

Stand with feet apart and parallel; arms extended to the sides.

COUNTS	MOVEMENT
1–2	Bend both knees.
3–4	Lift left heel off the floor and turn left knee in to face right knee, if possible, without moving the hips.
5–6	Return left heel to the floor as the left knee faces front again.
7–8	Straighten the legs.
9–16	Reverse—right foot.
17–32	Repeat counts 1–16 left and right.

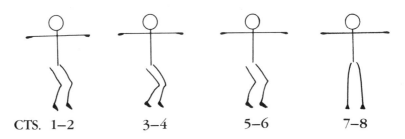

CTS. 1–2   3–4   5–6   7–8

NOTE: On counts 3–4, be sure not to roll over on the ankles. Keep the ball of the foot on the floor as you lift the heel up and turn the leg in.

5
jazz
arms

Arm movements could be considered as part of isolation movements; moreover, arms are a very important aspect of dancing. They add to the style, and they need to be emphasized and thought about. During the explanations of intricate steps and combinations, refer to this chapter for more specific and detailed instructions on arm movements. You may also wish to vary the arm movements used with the various steps when you know them well, so here you have a few from which to choose, unless you want to experiment and try new ones of your own. Sometimes you can get ideas just by watching people working, walking, or playing, which is exactly how many dance movements and jazz dance, too, evolved. So, vary what you do—try the arm movements with the suggested steps, and then with other walks that you will learn in Chapter 6, or do the steps and walks with your own different arm movements.

They need not always be practiced after the isolations. Begin your practice with some of the more easy, relaxed arm movements; or do them after bent legged walks, just to let your leg muscles stretch out long. You'll enjoy them. The solo photographs in the book are of steps covered in the book. You should be able to identify the movements shown once you have learned them. They have purposely not been placed near the description of the steps they represent.

jazz arms
(number 5–1)

ARM SWING AND SNAP
(FRONT AND BACK)

Use this movement with low level passé walk, No. 6–13, Chapter 6. Start with arms down at sides, feet slightly apart and parallel.

COUNTS	MOVEMENT
1	Swing arm forward in front of body in a nice, easy, relaxed manner. Head follows the movement of the left arm.
2	At the very top of that arm swing to the front, and just before dropping the arm down, snap the fingers and follow through by dropping the arm down at your side.
3	Continue the left arm swinging motion toward the back-left side direction in a relaxed manner, with the head following the down-and-up-toward-the-back direction that the arm takes.
4	At the very top of that arm swing toward the back-left side, and just before dropping the arm down, snap the fingers and follow through by dropping the arm down at your side.
5–16	Repeat 3 times.
17–32	Reverse counts 1–16.

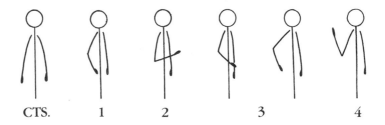

| CTS. | 1 | 2 | 3 | 4 |

NOTE: In this arm movement we can both see and hear syncopation—a basic characteristic of jazz and dance. On the offbeat, we can see the arm reach the very top of its swing, before dropping down, and we hear the fingers snap at that same instance.

jazz arms
(number 5–2)

ELBOW AND WRIST PRESSES
(FORWARD AND BACK)

Use this movement with camel walk, No. 6–19, Chapter 6. Start with arms down at sides, elbows bent, and palms facing down, slightly forward, and the wrist a bit flexed.

COUNTS	MOVEMENT
1	The right elbow moves forward and the left elbow moves backward about four inches each, with the rest of the arm in the same relative position as at the beginning—elbows bent and palms facing out with wrists flexed, so now the right palm faces forward and the left palm faces back or down. The palm is flat, with each finger close to the next one.
2	Reverse arms—left forward and right back.
3	Reverse arms again—right forward and left back.
4	Right elbow moves back about four inches from torso; left arm remains where it was—in back.
5–8	Reverse counts 1–4.
9–16	Repeat.

CTS.　1　　　2　　　3　　　+　　　4

NOTE: Jazz dance includes movements that are fluid and lyrical and also those that are very sharp and precise. In the above movement, the arms should be quick and precise, especially when done with the more syncopated camel walk (see No. 6–11, Chapter 6). It should then have the same energy-filled pauses that the leg action has.

jazz arms
(number 5-3)

JAZZ HANDS

Use this movement with isolations, grapevine, and high level passé walk, No. 4–2, Chapter 4; No. 6–9, Chapter 6; and No. 6–16, Chapter 6.

The hand is stretched out very wide from thumb to little finger. There should be a look and feeling of tension in the hand.

When used with grapevine or isolations, the arm is often extended out to the side with a sharp bend in the elbow. The hand is slightly higher than waist level, with the palm facing front.

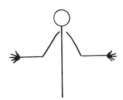

The jazz hand can also be used with the arm in a variety of other positions as desired. Try some yourself.

This tense, wide hand is a very strong-looking hand position that makes dance students very aware of their hands, how they are used, and the feeling they convey. It is not an easy hand position for beginners to maintain while doing a whole combination. Concentration is needed.

jazz arms
(number 5-4)

PALM PRESSES UPWARD

Use this movement with stretches and mambo square: No. 4–1, Chapter 4; and No. 10–4, Chapter 10. Start with arms down at sides.

COUNTS	MOVEMENT
1–2	Straighten right arm overhead and press right palm up toward the ceiling, with a flat palm and flexed wrist. At the same time, the left arm, overhead, is lower as the elbow bends slightly. The right side of the torso stretches up longer than the left side, which bends a bit toward the left.
3–4	Reverse.
5–16	Repeat 3 times.

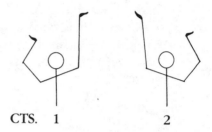

CTS. 1   2

jazz arms (number 5–5)

JAZZ HANDS FORWARD AND BACKWARD

Use this movement with high level passé walk, No. 6–16, Chapter 6.

Start with arms down at sides, elbows bent, palms facing each other. Hands are in jazz hand position (see No. 5–3).

COUNTS	MOVEMENT
1	The right elbow moves forward and the left elbow moves backward, about four inches each. The rest of the arm is in the same relative position as at the beginning—elbows bent and hands in tense, stretched jazz hand position.
2	Reverse arms—left forward and right one back.
3–8	Repeat 3 times.

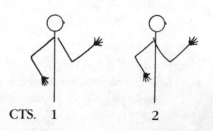

CTS. 1   2

jazz arms

jazz arms
(number 5–6)

ELBOW BENDING AT SIDES—ALTERNATELY

Use this movement with kimbos, No. 7–1, Chapter 7. Start with arms down at sides.

COUNTS   MOVEMENT

1   Bend right elbow in close to your side and raise lower arm until your hand is next to your shoulder. At the same time, tilt the torso and the head slightly to the right and bring the left shoulder slightly forward as the left arm drops down at the side.

2   Reverse.

3   Reverse quickly.

+   Reverse quickly.

4   Reverse.

5–8   Reverse counts 1–4 starting with left elbow bending.

9–16   Repeat.

CTS.   1   2   3   +   4

NOTE: This arm movement is essentially a very easy natural one. Many people would probably use it on their own, together with the slight torso bending to the side. However, they might not bend the lower arm up as far. Notice that the sketch is a mirror image of the text. The image in the sketch acts as a mirror image would; it faces you and bends its left arm when the text says right arm bends, on count 1, just as you would see in a mirror.

Photo by Clotilde

jazz arms
(number 5–7)

FLICK WRISTS FRONT AND BACK—ALTERNATELY

Use this movement with rhumba walk, No. 6–14, Chapter 6. Start with feet slightly apart, parallel, arms down at sides.

	COUNTS	MOVEMENT
Practice		

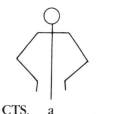

	a	Prepare to
	1	Lift shoulders up.
	+	Relax.

CTS.   a   1

Practice

	a	Prepare to
	1	Pulse-lift elbows up at the sides.
	+	Relax.

Practice

	a	Prepare to
	1	Bend straight long hands in at wrists with a slight outward lift or pulse of the wrist.
	+	Relax.

Practice All the Above Together

	a	Prepare to do all the above—shoulder, wrist, elbow, and hand movements—and to change arm positions; the front arm goes back and the back one goes front, all at the same time.
	1	Pulse elbows, shoulders, and wrists up slightly while flicking long hands in from wrists. At the same time, the torso rotates or twists slightly to the right if the right arm is front. The head looks over the left shoulder that has moved toward the front, as the left hand flicks up from the wrist, in back of you.

NOTE: East Indian hand and head movements have been used in jazz dance extensively. The long line from wrist to fingertips can be found in East Indian, Siamese, and Cambodian dances. For another similarly derived arm movement see No. 5-10.

jazz arms   87

jazz arms
(number 5–8)

DIAGONAL STRETCH, IN,
OVERHEAD, SIDE, ELBOW

Use this movement with jazz square and turn, No. 7–7, Chapter 7, and No. 8–5, Chapter 8. Start with arms extended out at sides.

COUNTS	MOVEMENT
1	Twist torso to the left, bringing the right arm forward and the left arm back. At the same time, tilt the torso down at the right side, so that the right shoulder is lower than the left shoulder.
2	Bend the elbows in close to you at the sides, with the lower arms touching the waistline at the sides. The hands are curled in a very loose fist, with palms facing up. Face straight front.
3	Right arm reaches directly overhead, moving up close to your side, and finishes straight up with the wrist highest. The fingers end the movement by dropping down from the wrist to the right.
4	Left arm reaches out directly to the side, shoulder height, and the fingers end the movement by dropping down from the wrist at the left side.
5	Bend the left arm over your head, so that the left hand is placed behind the right arm. Hold onto the right elbow.
6	Hold the position.
7–8	Extend arms out to the sides.
9–16	Reverse counts 1–8.
17–32	Repeat.

CTS.   1   2   3   4   5

jazz arms
(number 5–9)

ARM CIRCLING, ELBOW IN

Use this movement with pivot turn, No. 8–3, Chapter 8. Start with arms down at sides and held slightly away from body.

COUNTS   MOVEMENT

+   Rotate right arm inwardly at the right side so the palm faces to the right. Start to move the right arm down in front of the body and across to the left of your body, with the right shoulder coming slightly forward. Continue moving the right arm upward on the left side; the arm is somewhat rounded.

a   Continue moving the right arm, slightly rounded, overhead and to the right side. Torso and shoulders face directly front when arm is overhead.

1   Pull the right elbow in sharply, close to the waistline at the right side, with the elbow bent and the lower arm extending straight out to the right side, palm facing up. At the same time, the left shoulder comes slightly front and torso faces the front right corner.

2   Lower the arms down at the sides and face front.

3–4   Reverse—left arm.

5–16   Repeat 3 times.

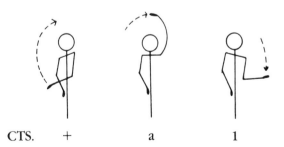

CTS.   +   a   1

NOTE: Make a large, wide arm movement as you circle the arm. Then finish it off with a sharp, quick pulling in of the elbow toward your waistline.

jazz arms
(number 5–10)

DRUMBEAT HANDS—UPWARD, DOWNWARD

Use this movement with hip presses side. No. 7–4, Chapter 7. Start with arms down at sides.

COUNTS	MOVEMENT
1	Lift straight arms overhead through sides. At the same time, the hands, from fingers to wrist, tap in as though beating a drum, with long hands and fingers—an unbroken line from wrists to fingertips, no knuckles showing. On the beat, the hands tap in toward the lower arms, with the palms facing up.
+	The hands go back from the wrists to be ready to tap forward again on the next beat, while continuing the upward motion of the straight arms through the sides.
2–8	Repeat the tapping hands 7 times as arms go up through the sides.
9–16	Repeat the tapping hands, with palms facing down now, as arms go down through the sides.

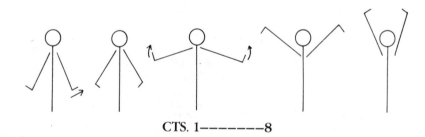

CTS. 1———————8

NOTE: Remember to keep the hands looking long and the action from the wrists only, not the knuckles.

6

jazz walks

One of the characteristics of jazz dance is the extensive use of low level movements. A movement that *does* reach away from the ground, as in jumps, some turns, slides, or extensions, provides a change of pace, but very quickly the movement will reach down into the ground again. There is a great variety of jazz walks, most of them done at low level, knees bent. It is a good idea, however, to alternate between these low level movements and other walks or movements that are not at low level; this is especially true for the beginning student, who will find the variety more restful.

Care should be taken to pull in the abdomen and lengthen the spine at the same time that the lower limbs go down into the floor. The knees should not be bent to their very lowest level, and the legs should have a feeling of elasticity. Remember that everyone is built differently. If you have a short tendon in the back of the heels, you will have to bend the knees less in order not to roll over on the inner border of the feet.

Another characteristic of jazz—use of body isolations—is evident in jazz walks. You will find descriptions of several jazz walks—some plain, then with an isolation of either the head, shoulder, ribcage, arm, or hip.

Many jazz movements have developed through improvisation. Have fun and add your own body isolations to some of the simpler jazz walks in this chapter.

jazz walks

Again, a reminder that the sketches are mirror images of the written descriptions. When the text says "step side on the right foot," the sketch faces you (like the mirror) and steps side on its left foot (just like the image facing you in the mirror).

jazz walks (number 6–1)

FLAT, LOW LEVEL

Stand with knees bent and feet slightly apart and parallel and arms down at sides.

COUNTS	MOVEMENT
1	Step forward on the right foot without lifting the foot off the floor, as though ironing the floor with your feet.
2	Reverse—left foot.
3–32	Repeat 15 times.

CTS.   1   2

NOTE: Pull up the abdomen; the feet press down and you pull up. Be sure the feet do not roll over. Do not bend the knees to their lowest point. Chin up, with the eyes focusing straight ahead.

This step shows the African influence on jazz dance, in the flat-footed step done with a gliding or dragging action, rather than actually lifting the foot off the ground. However, while African style favors the torso bent forward like a hunter ready to move, in this step the torso is held up high and tall, part of the native American heritage.

jazz walks
(number 6–2)

<u>HIGH LEVEL ON DEMI-POINTE</u>
<u>(BALLS OF THE FEET)</u>

Stand with feet parallel and arms down at sides.

COUNTS	MOVEMENT
1	Step forward on ball of right foot with knees straight.
2	Reverse.
3–32	Repeat 15 times.

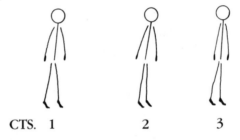

CTS.   1   2   3

NOTE: Keep knees very straight and thighs pulled up. Weight is very forward over the balls of the feet.

This step shows the influence of ballet on jazz—straight, taut legs stepping high on the balls of the feet, with body placement high over the hips. The steps that eventually are added into the domain of what is considered jazz dance, but were not in the earlier primitive jazz category, which included steps like the flat low level walk, probably reflect a need for visual and muscular contrast for dancer and audience, as well as individual preferences and trends. The use of a particular step or combination within the whole dance or production, together with the mood and music, is sometimes what makes it look more like jazz than like modern dance.

jazz walks
(number 6–3)

HIP LIFT SIDE, MOVING FORWARD

Start with feet slightly apart and parallel, knees bent with heels off the floor, arms extended out at sides (see No. 4–7, Chapter 4).

COUNTS	MOVEMENT
1	Step forward on the right foot with your weight well over that leg; at the same time lift the left hip up sideways.
2	Reverse.
3–32	Repeat 15 times.
32–64	Try it again, but with the heels on the floor. This step may be done either way—heels on or off the floor.

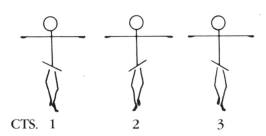

CTS.   1   2   3

NOTE: Be sure that the hip lift is in opposition to the forward foot. If you find it difficult to isolate the hip as you step forward, try doing 4 hip lift isolations first, to the left, right, left, right, then add the steps while going on with the hips (the right foot would be the first to step forward as the hips continue moving).

One of the characteristics of jazz dance, derived from African dance, is the use of the entire body in the dance. In African dance, the movement of the legs often seems to come as an impulse from a hip movement, rather than from the feet or the knees.

jazz walks
(number 6–4)

FLAT LOW LEVEL WITH HEAD SHIFT

Stand with knees bent and feet slightly apart and parallel and arms down at the sides (see No. 4–2, Chapter 4, and No. 6–1).

COUNTS   MOVEMENT

1   Step forward on the right foot without lifting the foot off the floor. At the same time, shift the head forward.

2   Reverse—step forward with the left foot. At the same time, shift head back.

3–32   Repeat 15 times.

CTS.   1   2   3

NOTE: Be sure not to vary the line of the torso. The head shifts forward; the shoulders and upper torso remain in place and do not move forward with the head.

This flat low level jazz walk is an excellent reminder that jazz dance goes down into the floor more than other dance forms and that originally in early, so-called primitive jazz, the steps were done with flat feet (whole foot on the floor) and bent knees. However, to compensate for this feeling of going down into the floor, one must, at first, perhaps, put more effort into pulling in the abdomen and thinking tall with a long erect spine. (The African dances from which jazz originated were, on the contrary, done with the upper torso bent slightly forward.)

jazz walks
(number 6–5)

TWIST—HIGH LEVEL

Stand with feet parallel and up on the balls of the feet, knees very straight. Arms are extended out to the sides (see No. 4–4, Chapter 4).

COUNTS	MOVEMENT
+	Pivot slightly to the left on the ball of the left foot. At the same time, lift the right foot, toes pointed, up to the knee of the left leg, so the right knee faces somewhat left.
1	Step forward diagonally left—farther front than the left leg is. The hips also twist to the left front corner, and the knees are both straight. Arms, head, and torso remain facing front, not left.
+2	Reverse—pivot on right foot and step on the left.
+3–16	Repeat 7 times.
17–32	Repeat twice as fast.

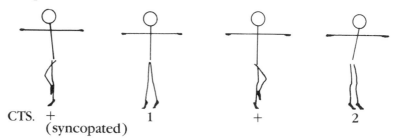

CTS.   +   1   +   2
   (syncopated)

For Advanced Beginners

For advanced beginners: When you know this step well, the counts will be as follows:

+	Pause, standing on the balls of the feet.
a	Lift foot up.
1	Step forward on the ball of the foot.

NOTE: Keep the weight very forward over the front leg. The legs should be very straight as you step. The legs and hips face diagonally right or left, while the head, arms, and torso face front.

jazz walks (number 6–6)

TWIST LOW LEVEL

Stand with feet parallel and knees bent, heels off the floor. Arms are extended out at sides (see No. 4–4, Chapter 4).

COUNTS	MOVEMENT
+	Pivot slightly to the left on the ball of the left foot. At the same time, lift the right foot slightly off the floor.
1	Step next to the left foot, on the ball of the right foot, with the knee bent, so that both knees are now facing diagonally left and the balls of the feet are parallel and close together. The arms are still extended at the side in their original position, and the upper torso remains front as much as possible. The hips twist to the left front diagonally along with the feet.
+2	Reverse—pivot on right foot and step on the left foot.
+3–16	Repeat 7 times.
17–32	Repeat twice as fast.

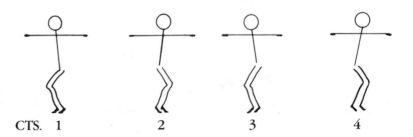

CTS.   1   2   3   4

NOTE: Take tiny steps without traveling much and keep the feet parallel as they face each diagonal—right and left. The foot that lifts and steps should feel as though it will turn in, not out, as you step on it. If you turn it out, you will probably end up by doing the Sugar Foot Walk (see Jazz Walk No. 6–17). Keep ankles and knees close together.

jazz walks
(number 6–7)

PASSE WALK LOW LEVEL—SLOW

Stand with feet parallel, knees slightly bent, and arms extended out to the sides.

COUNTS	MOVEMENT
1–2	Lift right foot, pointed, next to left leg, with the knee forward and turned out.
3–4	Put the ball of the right foot on the floor and slide the flat foot forward with the leg bent. Your weight moves forward.
5–8	Reverse—left leg.
9–32	Repeat 3 times.

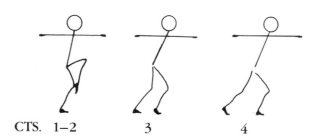

CTS. 1–2   3   4

NOTE: Hips should be parallel to the floor; do not lift the hip of the working leg. Bend the knees a comfortable amount, not to their lowest. Your center of gravity keeps moving forward constantly. Focus on a spot on the wall in front of you at eye level to help you to do the walk without varying your level by straightening your legs erroneously.

  The word *passé* comes from ballet terminology—the foot touches the knee and the leg is turned out. In the step described here, the foot is touching the knee or below, depending on one's ability, but the leg is not turned out; in fact, it is slightly turned in. The hips should be even, not one higher than the other. This is very important for beginners to remember as they practice.

jazz walks
(number 6–8)

HIGH LEVEL WITH SHOULDER ISOLATION

Stand with feet parallel and arms down at sides (see No. 4–3e, Chapter 4 and No. 6–2, Chapter 6).

COUNTS	MOVEMENT
1	Step forward on the ball of the right foot with the knees straight. At the same time, raise both shoulders.
2	Step forward on the ball of the left foot with the knees straight. At the same time, lower the shoulders.
3–32	Repeat 15 times.

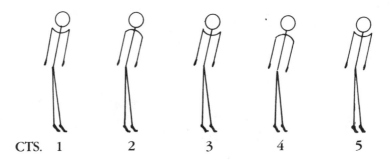

CTS.   1   2   3   4   5

NOTE: Keep the knees very straight and the thighs pulled up, especially as you lower the shoulders. The weight should be very forward over the balls of the feet.

jazz walks
(number 6–9)

GRAPEVINE

Stand with feet parallel, slightly bent knees. Arms extended to the sides with palms facing front, and fingers in a wide hand or jazz hand position. Elbows are approximately waist high and are held out away from the waist (see No. 5–3, Chapter 5).

COUNTS	MOVEMENT
1	Step to the side on right foot with slightly bent knee and a small amount of turnout.
2	Step front on left foot with bent knee and slight turnout.
3	Step side on right foot with bent knee and slight turnout.
4	Step back on left foot with bent knee and slight turnout.
5–16	Repeat 3 times as you continue traveling sideways.

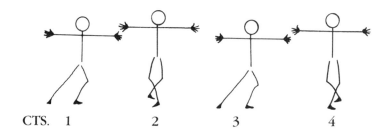

CTS.   1   2   3   4

NOTE: The grapevine is found in a variety of folk dances; also in ballet where it is called *pas de bourrée* and usually consists of three steps, starting either with a step crossing front or back. In folk dances, or tap, you often do a whole series of steps in this grapevine of steps, sometimes with a hip twist, sometimes without, but the steps start either to the front, side, or back, depending on the particular dance.

jazz walks
(number 6–10)

STEP IN ATTITUDE WITH CUTTING ARM

Start with feet slightly apart and parallel, arms extended out at sides.

COUNTS	MOVEMENT
1–2	Step forward on the left leg with a bent knee. As you lift the right leg up in back without turning it out, be sure to point the toes and keep the hips even—parallel to the floor without raising one higher than the other. The torso leans forward, as it usually does when a leg is raised in back. At the same time, cut across in front with the right arm, elbow slightly bent and palm up. You should feel as though the elbow initiates the movement. The torso leans a bit to the right.
3–4	Now the torso leans a bit to the left as the arm reverses its direction and moves from in front of you out to the side— again with the elbow leading the movement, but now with the palm facing down.
+	The right foot goes down and slides forward so you can reverse.
5–8	Reverse counts 1–4.
9–32	Repeat 3 times.

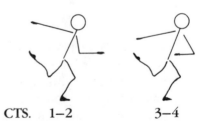

CTS.   1–2   3–4

NOTE: Keep the body weight well forward over the ball of the front foot on counts 1–3.

The attitude back position takes its name from ballet, but it is actually a very old, well-known position. It dates back to the statues of Mercury, who was a messenger for the gods as well as the god of commerce, eloquence, and thieves.

CAMEL WALK

Stand with feet together and parallel, arms down at sides.

COUNTS	MOVEMENT
1	Press right foot slightly forward, pressing right heel down into the floor until the heel of the right flat foot is next to the instep of the left foot. Immediately lift the heel of the left foot off the floor, with the left knee bending sharply in front.
2	Press the left heel into the floor and forward until the heel of the left flat foot is next to the right instep. Immediately lift the right heel off the floor with the right knee bending sharply to the front. The weight should be slightly back on the heels in the camel walk.

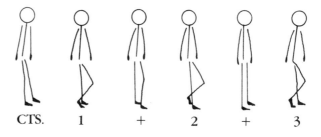

CTS.   1   +   2   +   3

For Advanced Beginners:

When you know this step well, the rhythm will be as follows:

+	Pause.
a	Press foot forward. (Syncopation, see No. 6-12 NOTE.)
1	Quickly lift the other heel as high as possible with the ball of that foot on the floor.

jazz walks
(number 6–12)

<u>STEP TAP, OFFBEAT CLAPS</u>
<u>AND HIP LIFT SIDE</u>

Stand with feet parallel and slightly bent, arms out at sides.

COUNTS	MOVEMENT
1	Step forward on left foot with knee bent; at the same time, clap hands.
2	Tap right foot side, at the same time lifting the hips up to the right side (see No. 4–7, Chapter 4). Clap hands also.
3–4	Reverse counts 1–2.
5	Step forward on left foot with knee bent.
+a	Clap hands in front twice.
6	Tap right foot side, while lifting the hips up to the right side.
+	Clap hands in front once.
7+a8+	Reverse counts 5+a6+.
9–16	Repeat counts 1–8.

<u>More Practice:</u>

If you cannot do the offbeat claps of counts 5–8, try it this way, very slowly: Say *"Hey,* Baba *Ree* Ba!"

1.	Step forward on left foot with knee bent and arms extended out to the sides: Say "Hey!"
+a	Clap hands in front twice: Say "BaBa."
2	Tap right foot side, at the same time lifting the hips up to the right side and with the arms extended out to the sides: Say "Re."
+	Clap hands in front once: Say "Ba."

Use any ditty that helps you to remember the rhythm; "Sunday It's Chicken," or "Meat and Potatoes" are others with the same rhythm.

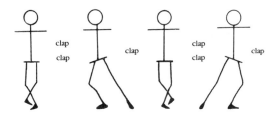

NOTE: Syncopation is a very important characteristic of jazz music and dance. In this step we can hear it very clearly on counts 5–8 as we put the accent on the offbeat each time we clap. Practice it with music and listen to the beat of the music in order to clap on the offbeat.

Do not listen to the claps, or they will stop feeling like offbeat claps. At this point, in order to have your clap sound like an offbeat clap, if you are in a group, you will start to clap on the offbeat of the other claps, which will be right on the beat of the music, not *on the offbeat* of the music.

A second kind of syncopation, more subtle, perhaps, can be used in many jazz movements and walks (No. 6-1 through 6-8 and 6-11). For people who can't seem to get the hang of it, here is a solution. If you have to get to a certain position on count 2, for example, don't start on count 1; anyone can do that! Start as late as possible and then rush the movement; get there on time , not a split second later. It makes the movement syncopated and exciting. It is very simple, if you can remember to do it, and it is not a matter of exaggerating a movement nor of increasing the amount of movement you do. Just start late, rush, and get there right on the beat

For most information on syncopation, see the Index.

jazz walks
(number 6–13)

PASSÉ WALKS—LOW LEVEL—
ACCENT ON DOWNBEAT

Stand with feet parallel slightly bent and arms down at to sides (see No. 6–7).

COUNTS	MOVEMENT
+	Pause
a	Lift left foot, pointed, next to right leg.
1a	Step forward on left foot, placing the ball of the foot on the floor and sliding the flat foot forward with the leg bent. Your weight moves forward throughout. As your weight continues moving forward over the front leg, the right arm swings down and across in front (see No. 5–1, Chapter 5).
+	Snap fingers of right hand across to left and turn head and torso slightly to left.
a2a+	Reverse—right foot. At the same time, swing right arm down and slightly back of side and snap fingers as head looks back to the right and torso twists slightly to the right.
a3–16a+	Repeat 7 times.
17–32	Reverse to other side with right foot starting and left arm swinging and snapping.

CTS.	a	1	a	+	a	2	a	+

NOTE: Only one arm does the swing and snap motion to the front and to the side back. The other arm remains down at the side.

jazz walks (number 6–14)

CUBAN OR RHUMBA WALK

Feet together; straight knees, weight slightly back on the heels, and arms down at sides.

COUNTS	MOVEMENT
1	Small step forward on the right foot with the knee slightly bent; press the top of the opposite hip out to the left side, keeping that back left leg straight and the weight somewhat back over the back leg, instead of the usual forward placement. At the same time, the left arm comes in front and the right one in back in opposition to the legs. The right shoulder comes slightly forward and up and the head looks over the right shoulder a little higher than eye level (see No. 4–7, Chapter 4, and No. 5–7, Chapter 5).
2	Reverse—left foot, right hip out to the side, weight back. Right leg straight and left slightly bent; right arm forward and left arm back. The shoulder of the back arm, or the left one, is slightly forward and up; head looks back over left shoulder.
3–16	Repeat 7 times.

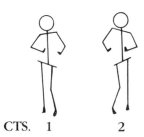

CTS.   1   2

NOTE: This is not the easiest step, so do it first with just the feet, then add the arms, shoulders, and head. Be sure to take small steps and keep the weight back so that the back leg can remain straight.

The rhumba is a Cuban dance that combines motifs of slave and Spanish folk dance. The woman's ruffled skirt and the man's ruffled shirt of colorful material, together with their steps, originally imitated the courtship dance of barnyard fowls.

jazz walks
(number 6–15)

STEP BALL CHANGE

Start with feet slightly apart and parallel. Knees are bent with heels on the floor, arms down at the sides (see No. 7–3, Chapter 7).

COUNTS	MOVEMENT
a	Lift right foot, pointed, next to left calf.
1	Slide-step forward on the toe, then the heel of the right foot. At the same time, bring left arm forward and carry your weight forward over the right leg. Right arm is extended out at side.
+	Pause.
a2	Ball change (step back on left foot with bent knee and quickly step forward on the right foot with bent knee).
+	Pause.
a3 + a4	Reverse.
a5–16	Repeat 3 times.

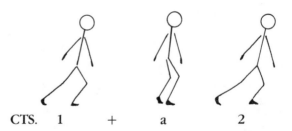

CTS.   1   +   a   2

NOTE: Many people who have done either tap dancing or social dancing (cha-cha and so on) will find this step somewhat familiar, except for the more precise way of lifting the foot at the beginning—pointed and next to the calf of the other leg.

jazz walk (number 6-16)

PASSÉ WALK—HIGH LEVEL

Start with feet slightly apart and parallel, arms down at sides.

COUNTS	MOVEMENT
a	Lift right foot up close to calf of left leg with foot pointing and left arm forward. Elbows are bent in at sides. Right arm is back, also with elbow bent. (Arms move, with bent elbows, from back to front or vice versa in a straight line each, as though on railroad tracks.) Jazz hands are used—fingers spread wide with palms facing as follows: right palm faces left, and left palm faces right (see No. 5–3, 5–5, Chapter 5).
1	Step forward high on ball of foot with a straight standing leg.
+2+	Pause in the above position. Upper torso is held slightly in front of the hips.
a3+4+	Reverse.
5–32	Repeat 7 times.

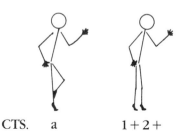

CTS.   a   1+2+

NOTE: Be sure that the movements are done sharply. The standing legs should be very pulled up and straight with the body weight well forward in order to be able to hold the legs straight while on the balls of the feet, the hips pressed back, with a flat back.

In this step we see the ballet influence of very straight, taut legs on a high demi-pointe (balls of the feet). However, the jazz influence is apparent in the hips pressing back, with the forward lean of the torso to counterbalance this, with the flat back position, as well as in the syncopation of the rhythm.

jazz walks
(number 6-17)

SUGAR FOOT

Stand with feet parallel and knees slightly bent. Arms are bent at sides with palms forward and elbows down. Heels are slightly off the floor. Palms are higher than the elbows.

COUNTS	MOVEMENT
+	Pivot slightly in, to the right on the ball of the left foot. At the same time, lift the right foot slightly off the floor.
1	Turn out the right foot and step forward on it on the ball of the foot, with the heel just slightly off the floor. The elbows are bent at the sides; the same palm as foot—the right palm—presses forward. The left elbow goes back a bit. There is an oppositional twist in the shoulders and upper torso—the right shoulder goes back and the left goes forward. Head remains front.
+2	Reverse.
+3–16	Repeat 7 times.

CTS.   1   2   3   4

NOTE: Remember that if you step forward, turned out on the right foot, the right palm presses forward. The torso and shoulders seem to take care of themselves. Most people will press the correct palm forward without much thought or practice being necessary.

A song and dance called "The Sugar Foot Stomp" was published in 1926 (music by Joseph "King" Oliver, lyrics by Walter Melrose, copyright owner Edwin H. Morris and Co., Inc.). In the 1920s, there were many, many pieces of sheet music published to all the new and so-called new dances going around. Many, like the "Sugar Foot Stomp," had words giving either general or precise directions on how to do the dance. "Walkin' the Dog" by Shelton Brooks is another example of this type of song for which dance and song lyric sheets were often handed out to the public to promote the latest songs and dances of the 1920s. There are dance directions throughout the lyrics, but they sound much like square dance calls (the more difficult to decipher, not the easier ones!)—if you know what they mean, then you know the dance; if you don't know what they mean, you can't do the dance (unless someone shows it to you).

jazz walks (number 6-18)

SKIMMING STEP BALL CHANGE

Start with feet slightly apart and parallel; knees bent; arms extended at sides (see No. 7–3, Chapter 7).

COUNTS	MOVEMENT
1	Slide right foot forward with a slight turnout, bent knee, and carry your weight forward over it. Left arm comes forward and right arm side (think "right foot starts, arms go right"). The above movement keeps going forward—the arms continue moving and the weight continues traveling forward. Try it first with arms extended out at the sides. With a slight lift off the floor, bring the left foot in back of the right foot on the ball of the foot.
2	Slide right foot forward again, going down into the floor.
3 + 4	Reverse.
5–16	Repeat 3 times.

CTS.   1   +   2

NOTE: This step has a lighter, springier quality than the "step ball change," which goes down into the floor.

This step is very similar to a ballet "chasse changé." It has the same light, airy quality; it skims across the floor instead of going down into the floor with weight—a good step for a change of pace from other walks that have more pronounced bent knees.

jazz walks
(number 6-19)

CAMEL WALK WITH ARM ISOLATION

Stand with feet together and parallel. Arms down at sides, elbows bent and palms facing down (see No. 5–2, Chapter 5, and No. 6–11).

COUNTS	MOVEMENT
1	As the right foot presses forward from the heel and the left heel raises off the floor, causing the left knee to bend, the right elbow moves forward and the left elbow moves back—about four inches each—with the rest of the arm in the same relative position as at the beginning, elbow bent and palm down. Do it with the arms down at the sides at first, to get the feel of the rhythm in the feet.
2	Reverse arms—left forward and right back. Reverse feet—press left forward and raise right heel.
3	Reverse arms—right forward and left back. Reverse feet—press right foot forward and raise left heel.
+	Right elbow only moves back about 4 inches from torso. The feet and left arm remain as on count 3.
4	Right elbow only moves forward about 4 inches from torso. The foot and left arm remain as on count 3.
5–8	Reverse—left foot and left arm.
9–32	Repeat counts 1-8, 3 times.

CTS.   +   1   2   3   +   4

NOTE: The weight is somewhat back on the heels. The feet move only on the first three counts of every four counts. The footwork should be smooth.

Years back the Camel Walk was a popular dance in minstrel shows.

7
jazz
center steps

This chapter includes jazz steps to be done more or less in place. You can see the derivation of jazz dance through many of these steps. Several come from earlier social dances—Suzie-Q and Black Bottom. Others are derived from later social dances of Latin influence, such as the mambo and the cha-cha; from later social dances we also have the lindy step. We see the folk dance influence in the grapevine and the tap influence in the ball change. Several of these center steps have syncopation and isolations. Many go down into the floor. These are all characteristics of jazz. But for a change of pace, and because dancers and choreographers keep adding other movements to jazz dance and experimenting, we also have a few steps that do not go down into the floor very much. This variety, which is what jazz dance consists of, is probably made more obvious in this same chapter than in other sections of the book. Bear in mind that the sketches mirror-image the description of the steps. They face you and move to their left as you move to your right, much as your mirror image does. The photographs are a quiz. Can you identify the steps shown in them? Have you looked up any of the excellent jazz dance, music, or dance history books mentioned in the bibliography? If you are practicing at home you might want to consider taking classes. See listing of excellent studios, in all areas, in *Dance Magazine*.

jazz center steps (number 7-1)

KIMBO

Start with knees bent, feet parallel. Do not rise up to middle level while doing kimbos. Arms are down at sides.

COUNTS	MOVEMENT
1	Step back on right flat foot with right knee bent. At the same time, the heel of the left foot remains in front on the floor, exactly where it was, and the toes of the left foot come off the floor as the left leg turns out to face the left wall. The torso bends slightly forward and to the left. The left arm bends up at the elbow; the elbow remains next to the body at the side; the right arm hangs down straight at the side (see No. 5–6, Chapter 5).
2	Reverse. The movement travels back, so allow sufficient space in back of you.
3–12	Repeat 5 times.

NOTE: The front leg remains straight and the body level does not change. This is easy to do since the lower torso presses out to the back. Remember to step back with a good-sized step on count 1, so that the heel of the front leg will be in front of you the correct distance and you will not have to lift the foot off the floor as it extends to the front.

jazz center steps
(number 7-2)

STEP FORWARD, BACK

For this cha-cha variation, stand with feet slightly apart and parallel, arms extended out to the sides, relaxed.

COUNTS	MOVEMENT
1	Step forward on right flat foot with knee bent and weight forward over the right foot.
+2	Two steps back (left, right) on the balls of the feet with *straight legs*. The weight remains slightly forward of the feet, or, rather, think of your head and upper torso remaining in the same place as on count 1 (forward), as your feet go back for counts +2.
3+4	Reverse.
5–16	Repeat 3 times.

CTS.   1   +   2

NOTE: In 1950, the mambo and all its variations gained popularity in the United States. One of these variations, the triple mambo, had fast footwork; as the soles of the shoes slid across the floor, sounds of cha-cha-cha could be heard, and the triple mambo became known as the cha-cha for short. It soon surpassed the mambo in popularity. It has a syncopated rhythm, and variations found their way into jazz dance combinations in class and on stage. The step described here, like many jazz steps derived from various sources, is not completely similar to its original version, but is an adaptation of it.

jazz center steps (number 7-3)

BALL CHANGE

Start with feet slightly apart and parallel, arms down at sides.

COUNTS	MOVEMENT
+	Ball change back-front. Step back on right foot, keeping the weight forward on the right foot, not on the back foot.
1	Step forward on the left foot, in place, or under you. (These 2 steps are like a catch step and the weight remains forward.)
+2–4	Repeat 3 times.
+	Ball change side-side: step on right foot, but do not transfer all the weight over the right foot and do not bring the body over the right foot, so the body and most of its weight remains over the second foot, or the left foot.
5	Step in place, under you, with the left foot.
+6–8	Repeat counts + and 5 3 times.
9–10	Pause.
11–18	Reverse back-front and side-side ball change, counts 1–8.

NOTE: Years ago, slaves (and later, convicts) were often seen laboring outdoors on roads, each with a heavy ball tied to one foot by a short chain. This meant that they could not change their weight very easily. When they did, it was a very quick step on the free foot and another short quick step close to the ground, on the foot tied to the ball and chain. These two steps became known as "ball change," now a very common step in both tap and jazz dance. It is often done on the balls of the feet in tap dance.

jazz center steps (number 7-4)

DRUMBEAT HANDS WITH HIP PRESSES

Start with weight on straight right leg; left leg has ball of the foot on the floor next to the right foot, with left knee bent and left knee overlapping in front of right leg; arms extended low side.

COUNTS	MOVEMENT
+	Lift hips up to left, and prepare the hands for the drumbeat motion by flexing them back at the wrist.
1	Press hips down and out to the right; at the same time use drumbeat hands (see No. 5–10, Chapter 5) and lift the arms from low side (through the side) to high side gradually, during counts 1–8.
+2–8	Repeat hip movement (lift and press) and arm and hand movement.
9–16	Continue the same hip movement (lift and press); reverse the arm movement (lower the arms down through the sides with drumbeat hand movement).
17–32	Repeat counts 1–16.
33–34	Get ready to reverse the hip movement.
35–66	Reverse counts 1–32 (arms remain the same; hips reverse).

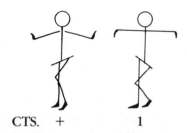

CTS.   +   1

NOTE: Hip presses are similar to the isolation movement of lifting the hip up to the side, except that in hip presses the hip lift is unaccented. The accent comes as the hip returns down past center and presses out to the other side.

jazz center steps (number 7-5)

GRAPEVINE KICK

Start with feet slightly apart and parallel; arms are extended to the sides with jazz hands (see No. 5–3, Chapter 5, and No. 6–9, Chapter 6).

COUNTS	MOVEMENT
1	Left foot steps across in back of right foot, with bent knee.
2	Right foot steps side with bent knee.
3	Left foot steps forward in front of right foot with bent knee.
4	Kick right foot front to right front corner (DSR—down stage right). The whole body faces that corner.
5–8	Reverse.
9–32	Repeat 3 times.

CTS.   1   2   3   4

NOTE: As your extension gets better, from doing all the warm-up exercises, you may kick the leg higher, providing you are still maintaining proper alignment. Leave the hips in place; do not tuck under while kicking. On the kick, be sure to keep the weight forward over the standing leg.

The grapevine twist was another dance that became famous in minstrel shows.

jazz center steps
(number 7-6)

SUZIE-Q, ONE FOOT

Both knees are bent. Stand on right foot with left foot lifted, pointed, touching the side of the right calf. Arms are bent in front of the torso, palms facing front, and elbows down.

COUNTS	MOVEMENT
1	Pivot on the right heel, lifting the toes, and place the toes out to the right side. Hands are still in front, palms forward, and both move slightly toward the left side.
2	Pivot on the right toes, lifting the heel, and place the heel out to the right side, turning the leg in. Both hands are still in front and move slightly toward the right side.
3–16	Repeat 7 times while traveling sideways.
17–32	Reverse—standing on left foot and traveling to the left side.

CTS.   1   2   3   4

NOTE: Remember to balance in the center of the triangle formed by your foot. Hold the ankle steady and do not roll over on either border of the foot as you place the toes or the heel on the floor. The arms move easily in natural opposition to the foot movement. The torso remains front, and the hips follow the movement of the legs.

The original Suzie-Q was a very popular social dance of the 1920s. This is an adaptation of one of its steps. It is usually done with two feet on the floor, but like many dances it lends itself to individual variations. (You can find other steps from the Suzie-Q in Joe Bonomo's *Learn the New Dances!* New York: Bonomo Culture Institute, 1953, 1962, p. 33).

jazz center steps
(number 7-7)

JAZZ SQUARE

Start with feet slightly apart and parallel, and arms out to the sides.

COUNTS	MOVEMENT
1	Step right foot crossed front of left, close to it, with straight right leg. The left back leg may bend slightly; at the same time arms are extended—the right arm diagonally forward low and the left diagonally back high, with the torso bending slightly forward and also tilting to the right (see Jazz arms, No. 5–8, Chapter 5).
2	Step directly back with left foot, with a relaxed knee. At the same time, the arms come in at the sides, the elbows bend in close to you at sides. The torso faces front.
3	Step side on right leg with relaxed knee; at the same time, right arm reaches high overhead with the wrist high and the fingers hanging down from it toward the side (not front).
4	Left leg steps front, forward of right leg with relaxed knee (not taut). At the same time, left arm extends out to the left side.
5–16	Repeat 3 times.
17–32	Reverse.

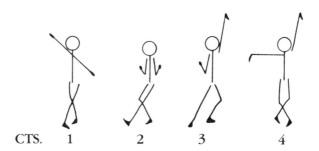

CTS.　　1　　　　2　　　　3　　　　4

NOTE: This step is always called a jazz square because, as you can see, the four steps outline the four corners of a square: front left corner, back left corner, back right corner, and then the front right corner of a square.

jazz center steps
(number 7-8)

MAMBO

Start with feet parallel and arms down at sides.

COUNTS	MOVEMENT
1	Step side on right foot with the right leg straight, the right hip pressing out to the right side, and the flat foot on the floor, either parallel to the other foot or slightly turned in. The torso bends to the left and the lower left arm bends up at the elbow as the right arm hangs down straight. The left leg is slightly bent.
2	Right foot steps in place next to the left foot. At the same time, the torso straightens up and the two elbows are held in at the sides, with the arms bent. Both knees are now relaxed.
3–4	Reverse with left foot.
5–16	Repeat 3 times.

CTS. 1   2   3   4

NOTE: As the right foot steps out to the side, with the right hip pressed out to the side, that leg is straight, but the left leg is slightly bent in place.

The mambo rhythm has been given various derivations: it is a syncopation of dances done by sugarcane cutters and is of Cuban-Afro origin; or, Puerto Ricans, fascinated by the movement of anchored boats rocking to and fro in the sea, started to bend and lift their bodies, hips swaying, in imitation of the movements of the water and the boats; or, it is derived from the Congo of Africa and the Shango of Trinidad. Tourists soon picked up the dance, and it became popular in the United States in the 1950s. It is fairly simple to do, with a jerky rhythm and a hesitation between steps. There are single, double, and triple variations in rhythm, all well liked. It was used very effectively as a jazz mambo in the Broadway musical *Damn Yankees,* choreography by Bob Fosse, in 1955.

8
jazz turns

Jazz turns are characteristically low level, on the balls of the feet and with the knees bent. But, for variety, they may be done high with a straight standing leg. This chapter includes an inside turn (to the right on the right leg—you feel as though you are turning in toward your center); an outside turn (to the right on the left leg—you feel as though you are turning away from your center); and a pivot turn—two feet swiveling on the floor, in place, causing you to turn somewhat. A more advanced turn (inside or outside), using the first or second turns taught in this chapter, starts high on the ball of the foot with a straight leg and then gradually the level of the body is lowered by bending the standing knee and continuing to turn. Before you try any steps at home, especially turns, look around to be sure you have sufficient space for all your movements, including the arms. Next, check the floor—neither too slick, nor too sticky. Then you're ready to start!

Once more, remember that the sketches in the book mirror-image the text, but you should learn the turning steps carefully so you do not have to look at the sketch or the text as you attempt to turn, if you are practicing at home.

jazz turns (number 8-1)

OUTSIDE LOW LEVEL

Start with feet slightly apart and parallel, and arms extended out to the sides.

<u>Practice First Without a Turn</u>

COUNTS	MOVEMENT
1–2	Step side on the right foot with a straight leg and with arms extended out to the sides.
3–4	Step back on the left foot with a bent knee. At the same time, bend the knee of front right leg, keeping the body weight over the front foot.
5–6	Lift the back left foot, pointed, next to the side of the right calf, bring the knuckles together in front with the elbows out to the sides, shoulder height. At the same time, lift the right heel slightly off the floor and balance in this position.
7–8	Close the left foot next to the right foot with both knees bent.

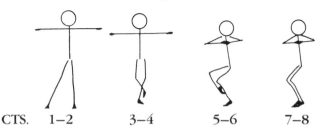

CTS.   1–2   3–4   5–6   7–8

<u>Now With a Turn</u>

9–10	Repeat counts 1 and 2.
11–12	Repeat counts 3 and 4.
13–14	Same as in the preparation for the turn on counts 5 and 6, but, as the right arm comes in front, let it push the whole body around. Feel as though the arm is connected to your whole torso and upper back area, so that when it moves to the left, your entire body turns to the left. Try to coordinate this arm movement with the left foot pushing off the floor as it comes up next to the right leg. Be sure to keep the torso forward, so your shoulders are over or slightly in front of your hips. The arm movement starts to push you around a split second before it is joined by the foot pushing off the floor.
15–16	Close the left foot next to the right foot with both knees bent.
17–64	Repeat 3 times (same pattern; 1 time without a turn, then 1 time with a turn).
65–68	Pause.
69–132	Reverse counts 1–64.

jazz turns

jazz turns
(number 8–2)

INSIDE, LOW LEVEL

Start with the weight on the right foot, right knee bent, left foot pointing on the floor to the side, and arms extended out to the sides.

COUNTS	MOVEMENT

Practice First Without the Turn

1–2   Bring left foot, pointing, to the side of the right calf. At the same time, bring knuckles together in front and elbows out to the side, shoulder height. Lift the right heel slightly off the floor.

3   Lower the heel of the right foot.

4   Point the left foot on the floor to the side.

Now With the Turn

5–6   Same as counts 1–2 above, but use the left arm to help you to turn. As you bring the left arm in front, think of it as being connected to your whole upper torso and shoulder area, so that when the left arm moves, your whole body will also move and turn to the right. The head, however, should remain facing the front until the left shoulder has gone by. Then quickly turn the head so it faces front again before the right shoulder gets there, as you turn. This is called "spotting," because you focus on one spot as you turn.

7–8   Lower the heel of the right foot to the floor and point the left foot on the floor to the side.

9–32   Repeat 3 times, counts 1–8.

33–64   Reverse.

NOTE: Spotting is essential for good turns. It adds a sharp, bright quality to them; aids in not getting dizzy during multiple turns; and in traveling turns, it helps you to see where you are going, whether anything is in your way, and to get where you plan to go.

CTS.   1–2   3   4

jazz turns (number 8–3)

STEP SIDE, TURNED-IN LEG, PIVOT

Start with feet slightly apart and parallel; arms are extended out at sides.

COUNTS	MOVEMENT
1	Bend knees as you step side on ball of right foot with right leg turned in (see No. 4–14, Chapter 4). At the same time, bring the right shoulder forward, the right elbow rotates toward the front, and the palm is facing the right with the hand down low at the side. Upper torso remains facing front. Left arm is rounded with the hand held loosely at the side of the body.
+	Move the whole right arm in a circular clockwise manner— from low right side, crossing down and over to left (palm now down), overhead, and over to the right with palm up (see No. 5–9, Chapter 5).
2	The arm finishes its circular pattern by having the elbow bend sharply in, close to you at the right side, with the lower arm extending forward to down stage right (DSR), or the right front corner. You are now facing DSR, or the front right corner, because at the same time the body will have pivoted to the right from the balls of the feet, and both knees are now facing DSR. The weight is forward over the right leg; the knees are both bent; the heel of the right foot is now on the floor; and the left heel is off the floor. As you pivot, the weight is transferred from the left foot to the right foot. The left leg is now turned in slightly.
3–4	Pause and bring feet slightly apart and parallel as at beginning.
5–16	Repeat 3 times.
17–32	Pause.

NOTE: The body remains at the same level throughout—low level.

CTS. 1   +   2

jazz turns
(number 8-4)

<u>ATTITUDE TURN, INSIDE,</u>
<u>SHOULDER SHIMMY</u>

Before starting this turn, see No. 9–4, Chapter 9. Then begin with feet slightly apart and parallel, arms extended at sides.

COUNTS	MOVEMENT
1–2	Step forward on the left leg with a bent knee. As you lift the right leg up in back with a bent knee and no turnout, push that foot up from the floor, lean forward from the torso, and lift the heel of the standing leg slightly off the floor so that you can turn on the ball of the left bent leg. At the same time, cut across in front with the right arm, elbow slightly bent and palm up. Feel that the arm is connected to your whole torso and shoulder area and pulls you around to the left. (A turn to the left on the left foot is an "inside turn"; see No. 6–10, Chapter 6.)
3–4	Finish by facing the front left corner DSL (down stage left), and slide the right foot down, going next to the other foot and front so it points toward down stage left (DSL), or front left corner, with a bent knee. Standing leg is slightly bent and its heel is now down on the floor. Right palm is down, and both arms finish diagonally front side, shoulder height. Torso leans back slightly.
5–8	In the above position—torso leaning back and arms forward with palms down—shimmy both shoulders alternately back and front quickly (see No. 4–6, Chapter 4).
9–16	Reverse.
17–64	Repeat 3 times.

CTS. 5–8

NOTE: The shimmy should be done just with the shoulders; hips remain still. During the beginning of the turn, try to coordinate the foot pressing off the floor with the arm and shoulders pushing around to turn. During the turn, the torso leans forward and the body weight should be well over the standing foot. Remember to spot on each turn. Look at one spot in front of you, for as long as possible, without tilting the head, and quickly turn the head to look again at that same spot.

jazz turns
(number 8-5)

COMBINATION—JAZZ SQUARE,
HIGH OUTSIDE TURN, TWIST

Start with feet slightly apart and parallel, and arms extended at sides.

COUNTS	MOVEMENT
1–4	One jazz square (see No. 7–7, Chapter 7), crossing right foot front, left foot back, right foot side, and left foot front (for arms, see No. 5–8, Chapter 5).
5	One outside turn to the right on the left foot (see No. 8–1; this one is the same idea, but high level). Bring the right foot, pointed, up close to the side of the left calf. While lifting it, push the floor away to start your turn with impetus. The left leg is straight and up on the ball of the foot when you rise up to turn. At the same time, pull the spine up tall and bring the left hand in back of the right arm to clasp the back of the right elbow while turning. Keep the shoulders and torso either directly over the hips or slightly in front of them. Be sure to lean forward slightly. Right arm is directly overhead.
+	Finish the turn by opening the arms to the sides and bending the standing leg, right foot pointed, still next to the left calf.
6–8	Three low level twist walks (see No. 6–6, Chapter 6).
9–16	Reverse.

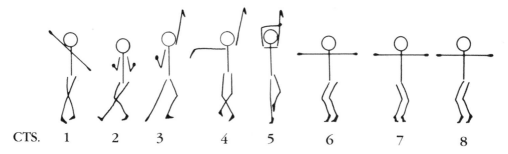

CTS.   1   2   3   4   5   6   7   8

NOTE: More advanced students may wish to try a double turn on one foot; you turn twice without stopping and without placing the foot down, or do a double turn with the first turn in high level and the second one in low level, with the knee bent and the standing heel slightly off the floor. This is more difficult. Remember to spot on the turn—look at one spot in front of you, as long as possible, without tilting the head, and quickly turn the head to look again at that same spot.

9

jazz combinations across the floor

Combinations across the floor are always great fun to do. One gets a sense of really covering space. If you are practicing these at home, be sure you really do have space for a combination. Walk it through slowly, then do it fully. These combinations include many smaller segments that have been explained in earlier chapters. Refer to those chapters for a quick refresher and helpful hints on execution. The better you know the movements, the more fun it is to do the combinations.

Once you know the combination well, you will want to add a little something extra—maybe a sharper movement or a slightly different rhythmic phrasing, a more pronounced accent or a slight pause and a quicker movement, or a lyrical flowing motion; so there is a bit of individuality in the dance combination when you perform it. When you know the combination, you can take a few liberties in phrasing, dynamics, and accents; you will still be doing the combination correctly, but with a touch of you in it. As you look at the photographs, you may notice some of this in them.

By now you have grown accustomed to looking at the sketches as you read, and you know that they mirror-image the text. This is the usual procedure for dance technique books. It facilitates your reading and trying out the sketch at the same time, without turning the book to face away from you.

jazz combinations across the floor
(number 9-1)

STEP, KICK, DIG,
KICK, GRAPEVINE

Start with feet slightly apart and parallel. Arms are extended out at sides, face front, and travel left to right (see No. 6–9, Chapter 6).

COUNTS	MOVEMENT
1	Step side on right foot.
2	Kick left leg forward so that it rebounds in from the knee immediately after the count of 2. (It's a flick kick.)
3	Toe dig left foot in place (ball of the left foot digs into the floor next to the other foot, without putting your complete weight on it).
4	Kick left foot diagonally side to front so the foot rebounds in from the knee immediately after the count of 4 (flick kick).
5–7	Grapevine to the right with arms extended at sides and relaxed hands, not jazz hands (step back on the left, side with the right, front with the left foot).
8	Pause.
9–32	Repeat 3 times.
33–64	Reverse counts 1–32.

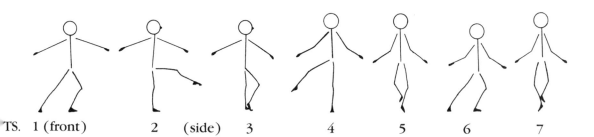

TS.   1 (front)   2   (side)   3   4   5   6   7

jazz combinations across the floor
(number 9-2)

<u>PASSE WALKS (LOW LEVEL),</u>
<u>RISE, AND ARCH</u>

Start with feet slightly apart and parallel; arms are extended out at sides.

COUNTS	MOVEMENT
a1 +	Passé walk (low level) forward with right foot (see No. 6–13, Chapter 6), arms extended out at sides (see also No. 6–7, Chapter 6).
a2 +	Passé walk (low level) forward with left foot.
a	Lift right foot close to calf of left leg, foot pointing.
3	Relevé (rise) on ball of left foot. At the same time, drop head forward and round the upper torso—shoulders and arms—so that the elbows are now facing the ceiling; arms are still out at sides. Practice this while standing on a flat foot at first.
+	Step forward on right foot, bent knee, and head and torso straight; arms side with elbows facing back, as is usual.
4	Lift left foot in back without turning out the leg, and arch the upper torso with the chest up, shoulders down, and the head back. Hands are in back of the hips.
+	Snap fingers back of hips while in the same position as in count 4.
5–8	Reverse.
9–16	Repeat counts 1-8.

CTS.   3   +   4

NOTE: Be careful to keep the shoulders down while arching the head and snapping fingers. See No. 4–11, Chapter 4, for better upper torso movements.

This combination shows the influence of modern dance in the rounding of the upper torso while on the ball of the foot. If the influence had been predominantly of African dance origin, the step would probably have been done with bent knees and heels on the floor as the torso rounded.

jazz combinations across the floor (number 9-3)

HIP LIFT WALKS,
ROLL, AND SNAPS

Start with feet slightly apart and parallel, elbows bent in at sides, close to the body.

COUNTS	MOVEMENT
1–8	Eight walks forward with a hip lift side in opposition. Right foot starts; (see No. 6–3, Chapter 6). Knees are slightly bent, heels off the floor.
9	One more step as above, with right foot.
10	Left foot steps next to right foot. All of the steps so far have been on the balls of the feet, knees bent slightly. This one is similar—up on the ball of the foot with knees bent.
11–12	Snap fingers 2 times.
13–14	Knee roll (left, front, right, center); see No. 4–10, Chapter 4.
15	Pause.
+	Snap fingers 1 time.
16	Snap fingers 1 time.
17–64	Repeat 3 times with a very tight, compact feeling.
65–128	Reverse.

CTS. 11–12 and 15–16

NOTE: These hip lift walks should have clear hip isolations; no extraneous movements of the upper torso should be added.

Photo by Clotilde

136

jazz combinations across the floor (number 9–4)

<u>ATTITUDE BACK WITH CUTTING ARMS; SHIMMY</u>

Start with feet slightly apart and parallel; arms are extended out to the sides (see No. 4–6, Chapter 4, and No. 6–10, Chapter 6).

COUNTS	MOVEMENT
1–2	Step forward on left leg with knee bent. At the same time lift the right leg up bent in back, without turning it out, keeping the hips level, horizontal to the floor. The right arm cuts across in front, right to left, with the palm up; elbow leads.
3–4	As the right arm now cuts across from left to right, palm down, the right foot goes down and slides forward along the floor until it is pointing front with both knees slightly bent. The right foot is pointing front toward the front left corner (DSL—down stage left). Now both arms are slightly front of side and the upper torso is leaning back a bit. Abdomen is pulled up.
5–8	In the above position—torso leaning back and arms almost front, with standing knee relaxed and right foot pointing toward the left front corner, shimmy the shoulders only (no hips) alternately backward and forward quickly. Keep a high arch in the torso.
9–16	Reverse.
17–32	Repeat counts 1–16.

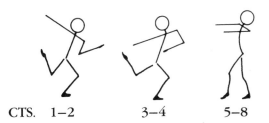

CTS.   1–2   3–4   5–8

NOTE: Keep the body weight well forward over the ball of the foot on counts 1 and 2. The torso should lean slightly forward. On counts 5–8, as you shimmy you may prefer having the arm that is closer toward the front or down stage (DS) slightly lower than the other arm; it makes a prettier picture.

jazz combinations across the floor (number 9–5)

RHUMBA WALK, CHA-CHA, TURNS, SHIMMY, SQUARE, TWIST

Start with feet slightly apart and parallel, and arms down at sides.

COUNTS	MOVEMENT
1–2	Two Rhumba walks (also called Cuban walks) starting with the right leg (see No. 5–7, Chapter 5, and No. 6–14, Chapter 6).
3–4	Step front, back, back—Cha-Cha variation (see No. 7–2, Chapter 7)—with the right, left, and right foot.
5–8	Reverse counts 1–4.
9–10	Attitude turn inside on right foot (see No. 6–10, Chapter 6, No. 8–4, Chapter 8, and No. 9–4).
11–12	Point foot front and shoulder shimmy.
13–16	Jazz square, crossing left foot front of right (see No. 5–8, Chapter 5, No. 7–7, Chapter 7, and No. 8–5, Chapter 8).
17–18	Single or double outside turn, high level, to the left on the right foot.
19–20	Three twist walks low level, or use counts 19–20 to finish your double turn from above counts 17–18, if necessary.
21–22	Three twist walks, low level (see No. 6–6, Chapter 6).
23–24	Three twist walks, low level.
25–32	Pause.
33–64	Reverse.
65–128	Repeat.

CTS.　　19　　　　+　　　　20

NOTE: The rhumba has always been a favorite of dancers. It appeared in the United States in the 1920s and was refined for more popular social dancing by the 1940s. Its popularity as a jazz dance movement can be attributed to its smooth, rhythmic, pulsing movements in the hips and throughout the whole body, along with the earthy feeling of the steps going down into the ground. Its heritage is Afro-Latin, with a touch of Indian and Spanish.

Rhumba rhythms have appeared in such shows as: *Earl Carroll's Vanities of 1930* ("Rhumba Rhythm" by J. Johnson and S. Unger); *Banjo Eyes,* 1941 ("Who Started the Rhumba" by Vernon Duke and John Latouche); *The Third Little Show,* 1931 ("When Yuba Plays the Rhumba On The Tuba" by Herman Hupfeld); and *Let's Face It,* 1941 ("A Little Rhumba Numba" by Cole Porter).

10
jazz combinations center

These jazz combinations include many steps that you have already learned. You will find notes such as "see No. 4–5, Chapter 4" to help you to locate the more detailed explanations of parts of the combination. Several of the combinations in this chapter do not have any such notes. They are more complicated steps than many of those previously explained and require more expertise to execute correctly. If you have carefully gone through the previous chapters and have been practicing on a regular basis, you should be ready for these. However, the easier center steps and the walks and turns in Chapters 6, 7, and 8 need to be reviewed, not by rote but with concentration and the intention of doing them better each time. Several of these combinations do require a lot of space, so try them slowly at first, being sure that you do have the space required. Look at the sketches (mirror images of the text) as you carefully read the text and walk through the combinations. Then get the book out of your hands; review the combination several times until it has "gotten into your bones." Then do it more rapidly, when you are sure of what you are doing.

jazz combinations center (number 10–1)

KIMBOS, HIPS UNDER

Start with feet slightly apart and parallel, and arms down at sides.

COUNTS   MOVEMENT

1–3   Three kimbos (see No. 7–1, Chapter 7), right, left, right— moving backward. (For arms, see No. 5–6, Chapter 5.)

+   Bend both knees and bring hips under yourself.

4   Bottom of the hips go back, and front leg straightens to same position as in kimbos. Arms remain as they were on the last kimbo.

5–8   Reverse.

9–16   Repeat counts 1–8.

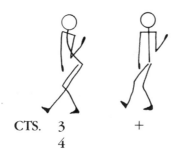

CTS.   3   +
           4

NOTE: You are getting the feel of jazz dance by now, and should try to see some professional dancing. TV offers "Solid Gold," "Dance Fever," wonderful reruns of movie musicals—"Flower Drum Song," "Cabaret," "Oklahoma," "West Side Story." On the live concert stage, see Gus Giordano's Company, Pepsi Bethel's Jazz Dance Company, Alvin Ailey's Dance Company. Ailey's repertory includes modern jazz dance: Talley Beatty's "Road of the Phoebe Snow," Donald McKayle's "Games," Alvin Ailey's "Mooche," and works by Katherine Dunham. Theater Development Fund plans on offering half-price tickets on day of performance—for Broadway shows at more locations in New York City; check for the one nearest you. Summer stock tents and road companies of Broadway shows also offer excellent dancing.

jazz combinations center (number 10–2)

KIMBO SPECIAL

Start with feet slightly apart and parallel, knees bent, and arms down at sides. You start at low level and remain there for this step.

COUNTS	MOVEMENT
1	One kimbo—step back on left foot with bent knee. At the same time, extend right leg front with the heel on the floor. Toes are off the floor and slightly turned out. The torso leans forward and to the right. The right elbow is bent in at the side and the left arm is straight down at the side (see No. 7–1, Chapter 7).
+	Bring right foot next to left foot, knees bent and feet flat on the floor, knees both facing diagonally to the left. Left elbow is bent in at the side, and right arm is straight down.
2	Step back again on left foot, with bent knee and right heel on floor, right toes off the floor, turned out. At the same time, the right elbow bends and the left arm is straight down at the side; the torso leans slightly forward and to the right.
3 + 4	Reverse—step back on right leg.
5–16	Repeat 3 times.

CTS.   1   +   2

jazz combinations center
(number 10–3)

MAMBO, RONDÉ DE JAMBE

Start with feet slightly apart and parallel, and arms extended out at sides.

COUNTS	MOVEMENT
1 + 2 +	Mambo left and right quickly (see No. 7–8, Chapter 7).
3 + 4	Grapevine (see No. 6–9, Chapter 6). Step cross left foot back, right foot side, left foot front, with arms extended out at sides and relaxed hands. (This could also be done with jazz hands.)
+ a	Kick right foot front to right front corner and your body faces there, too. Then do a quick rond de jambe en l'air before repeating counts 1–4. This is a circular movement, or a long oval shape made by the right leg. From the end of the kick, the leg circles forward and in toward yourself, and then slightly back as the leg extends out for the next mambo on count 5, with the hip reaching out to the side.
5–8	Reverse counts 1–4.
9–16	Repeat counts 1–8.

CTS. +   a   5

NOTE: A *rond de jambe* is a ballet term; like all ballet terminology, it is French. It means a circle of the leg; this one is *en l'air*—in the air. Ballet terminology is so well known by dancers that it is almost impossible not to refer to it as a simple means of explaining a step; its influence has been felt in all areas of dance. Actually, there are steps that look somewhat like a rond de jambe in other forms of dance, such as in African dances and in the cancan. The above jazz combination also reflects the variety of backgrounds in jazz dance: the social dances of Latin origin in the mambo, the European folk dance, and just about everybody in the grapevine and the kick.

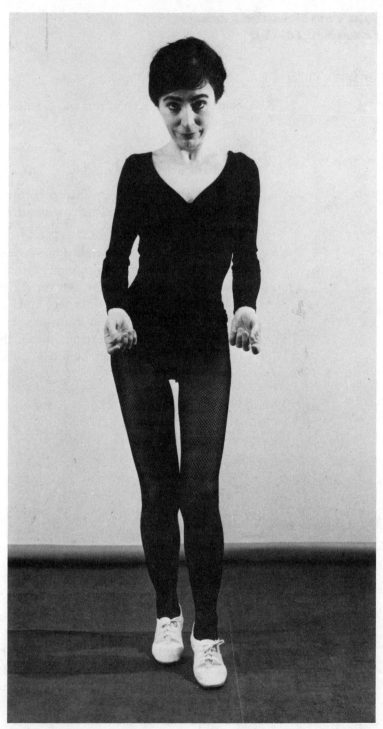

Photo by Clotilde

MAMBO SQUARE

Start with feet slightly apart and parallel, knees a bit bent, and arms down at sides.

COUNTS	MOVEMENT
1–4	Four palm presses overhead—right, left, right, left; 1 count each (see No. 4–1, Chapter 4, and No. 5–4, Chapter 5.)
5–8	Four kimbos backwards—1 count each (see No. 7–1, Chapter 7).
9–12	Mambo right and left; grapevine, kick front (see No. 7–8, Chapter 7).
13–16	Reverse counts 9–12—start left foot. During the grapevine do ¼ turn right to finish facing the right side, SR (stage right), for the kick forward toward SR.
17–32	Repeat counts 1–16 facing SR (stage right).
33–48	Repeat counts 1–16 facing the back of the room US (up stage).
49–64	Repeat counts 1–16 facing the left side of the room SL (stage left). The ¼ turn at the end will have you finishing facing DSF (down stage front).
65–68	Pause.
69–132	Reverse.

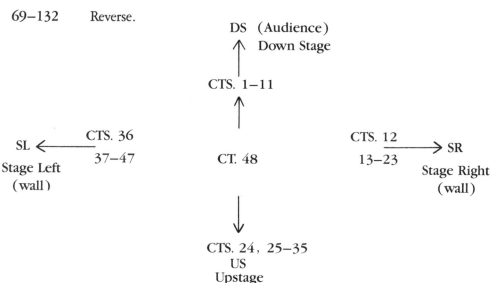

NOTE: This "mambo square" is a combination that the students in a beginners' jazz class put together as part of the "crocodile rock" routine (see No. 12–2, Chapter 12). They took the arm movements from the body stretches, used the kimbos, the mambo combination, and added a ¼ turn. The repetition is very agreeable since it has variety within the combination, and it feels good to do.

Years ago, stages were usually raked; if you walked toward the back of the stage you walked uphill, so it is called up stage (US); if you walked toward the audience you walked downhill, so this is called down stage (DS). Today, raked stages are a rarity, but they still exist; dancers must then get used to balancing themselves differently so they are at all times aligned over their feet at the correct angle with the raked floor; they must be able to move easily in any direction whether sideways, uphill, or downhill, regardless of the step, and do so with fluidity. Although raked stages are now rare, the name of the directions are still the same—DS (down stage), US (up stage), SR (stage right), and SL (stage left). The directions *right* and *left* are named according to the performer's right and left when on a proscenium stage, facing the audience.

jazz combination center (number 10–5)

STEP, KICK, TURN, SUZIE-Q

Start with feet slightly apart and parallel; face DSR (down stage right), or the front right corner. Arms are extended out to the sides, relaxed.

COUNTS	MOVEMENT
1	Step side on left foot with arms extended to the sides (see No. 9–1, Chapter 9).
2	Kick right foot front (to front right corner, which you are still facing).
3	Toe dig right foot (ball of right foot goes on the floor next to left foot, without a change of weight).
4	Kick right foot diagonally side.

5–7	Grapevine to the left (step back right foot, side left foot, front right foot). (See No. 9–1, Chapter 9, for more detail on counts 1–8.)
8+9	Step side on ball of left foot with left leg turned in, and pivot on both feet to face DSL (down stage left), or front left corner. At the same time, the left arm moves from down front, counter-clockwise to left, and then the elbow comes in at your side as you face the front left corner (see No. 8–3, Chapter 8).
10	The weight is now on the left front foot. Kick the right foot front toward DSL, or front left corner, with arms extended out to the sides, relaxed. Left knee is bent.
+	Bring right foot to side of left calf, foot pointed.
11	Point right foot side on floor. Left knee is bent; no turnout in right leg.
12–13	Inside turn to the left (see No. 8–2, Chapter 8). Right foot is up at side of left calf, pointed, and knuckles are together in front with elbows out at sides—shoulder height. Standing heel is slightly off the floor and knee is bent.
14	Lower the standing heel, bent knee, but do not lower right foot. (Do not turn out the standing leg and foot as you lower the heel, or you may have trouble starting Suzie-Qs that follow.)
15+16	Suzie-Q left on left foot with palms facing forward and elbows down, bent (see No. 7–6, Chapter 7).
+	Extend arms out to the sides with fingers hanging down from wrists (palms facing you).
17–32	Reverse.

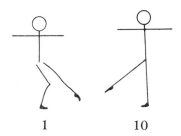

1   10

NOTE: When you know the combination well, do it more quickly but not lightly. Remember to step down into the floor with weightiness; pull in the abdomen and keep the movements sharp and concise. In this combination, you should feel as though the movements are pulling in toward you rather than reaching out.

Again, when you know the combination well, try it this way: on count 1, begin by facing the front right corner DSR (down stage right) instead of straight forward. In this way counts 1-7 will move on the diagonal. On count 10, face the front left corner DSL (down stage left). So, instead of facing forward, counts 1-8 face DSR and counts 9-16 face DSL. To reverse, face DSL on counts 1-8 and DSR on counts 9-16.

11 cooling down exercises

These are exercises to be done at the very end of the class. They have several purposes: to emphasize a previously done centered type of exercise; to relax and to cool down before leaving the class or the practice session; and to center the body before finishing the practice session. They are important in case you have been doing a combination in which the body is not "centered"—such as one with balancing on the same one foot several times, or with the same one hip doing a hip lift side, or the same one arm reaching back constantly. You may have practiced the combination several times in a row to the other side also, but alternating sides constantly is best. Now in these cooling down exercises, you get a chance to concentrate on yourself by using the easier-to-remember exercises, rather than getting involved with the complexity or newness of a step or combination. These are all very "square" types of exercises, with both sides of the body doing the same thing at the same time— simple and easy to remember.

These exercises might also be some of the very ones you wish to practice when you only have a few minutes to spare—perhaps at the beginning or end of the day. If you get in the habit of practicing a little but regularly, you soon find a few exercises that feel good on your body, and it is good to get back to them occasionally.

cooling down exercises
(number 11–1)

cooling down exercises
(number 11–2)

PASSIVE STRETCH AND RELAXING POSITION

On your back in hook lying position with knees bent, pointing up toward the ceiling, and the arms either extended out to the sides, like a T-bar, shoulder height or even higher if more comfortable, with palms facing up; relax the shoulders and the whole back down flat on the floor. The back and shoulders should eventually be able to flatten down on the floor for most people. This is a very good way to relax for a few minutes, if your back, shoulders, or neck gets tense, or just to rest when you finish your workout and practice session.

Don't forget, as you do this relaxing exercise, to open the mouth slightly and drop the jaw down to better relax the whole neck area. Imagine also that your eyes are very wide and extend from the right side of your head to the left side—marvelous for the eyes, face, and forehead. Yawn if you feel like it (even if you don't—it's also relaxing). If you are feeling tense or tight, this exercise should make you feel better. If you had a rough day or expect to have one, take just a 10-minute nap after the exercise. It can do wonders.

If you sit a lot, you might prefer relaxing on either your back or abdomen, with straight legs instead, to stretch your legs a bit at the same time that you relax.

cooling down exercises
(number 11–3)

SITUPS WITH FEET ON LEDGE

Start with the feet up on a low bench, chair, 3 large phone books or something of the sort. Torso is on the floor and arms overhead on the floor.

COUNTS	MOVEMENT
1–8	Pull up the thighs. Pull the abdomen in toward the center line and up. Press the waistline down on the floor. Pull the buttocks in toward your center line and up, and slowly roll up, leaving your feet up on the bench. (The bench, books, pillows, or chair are against the wall so they won't move as you press into them.) The arms are extended in front of you and the hips roll under as you roll up, so that one vertebrae after another rolls up off the floor—controlled and slowly—with a flat tummy. The hands and head then reach as far forward as possible toward your feet and knees.
9–16	Slowly reverse the process, and roll down one vertebrae after another with the hips under, until you are back on the floor. The abdomen, thighs, and buttocks are pulled up as before.
17–24	Now relax. Drop the jaw and relax your neck; relax your tummy, buttocks, and thighs. Lift your right arm up and drop it down limp; do the same with the left arm.
25	Repeat counts 1-24—start with 5 times the first day and do the same for 1 week. Next week start doing 10 a day for 3 weeks; then do 15 a day, every day for 3 weeks; then add 5 more—for a total of 20 a day—for the next 3 weeks; and do those every day at the end of your practice session, or when you only have a few minutes to spare.

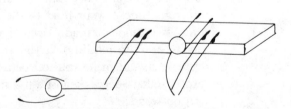

NOTE: If you do the above, you will do situps every day for ten weeks without skipping a day. And then you should start to feel that you have a nice firm tummy. (If there is still too much of it, eat a little less of what you usually eat—and do that regularly; you will lose weight.) You should also have firmer thighs and buttocks. If you feel your head, neck, or shoulders tightening, that is not good—spend more time on counts 17-24 and concentrate on relaxing between each situp. After about 6 months of this, gradually reduce the size of the ledge. For example, start with 3 large phone books; then after 6 months, use 2 large phone books; after 1 year, use only 1 large phone book; after 2 years, do them either on your bed or on a mat; after 3 years of doing them regularly, every day, do them on the floor, *but do them with your elbows on the floor.* Pull your tummy in and up; keep your feet and toes close together so the legs and thighs do not turn out. Leave the elbows on the floor so the back can relax and feel as though you are pouring it down on the floor and gently lifting it up off the floor, as you go down to the floor and as you come up. If your waistline and lower back are off the floor when you are flat on the floor, rather than relaxed flat into the floor, you should still be using a ledge for your feet while doing situps.

This particular situp is very good because no matter how your back, buttocks, or thighs are shaped, or how flexible or unflexible they are, you can do these correctly, with the tummy, not the lower back, doing the work, which is as it should be. If your legs are not comfortable when straight, or just to vary the exercise, keep them bent and place the calf and feet over the bench or book. Each vertebrae should touch the floor as you roll up and roll down. Place an open phone book, blanket, or cushion over your feet if they won't stay down.

cooling down exercises (number 11–4)

ALL OVER BODY STRETCH

Start with feet slightly apart and parallel, arms down at sides.

COUNTS	MOVEMENT
1–4	Starting with the head, slowly roll the torso downward; first the head, then the shoulders, upper torso, and lower torso, until you are as far down as possible with the arms relaxed, hanging down, relaxed, from the shoulders.
5–6	Arms and upper torso reach forward until the back is parallel to the floor and straight like a table top, with the arms forward, next to the ears. Head follows the line of the vertebrae.
7	Lift the torso up with arms straight overhead.
8	Lower the arms down through the sides.
9–10	Bend knees.
11–12	Straighten legs with a smooth, elastic motion.
13–14	Rise up on the balls of the feet.
15–16	Lower heels.

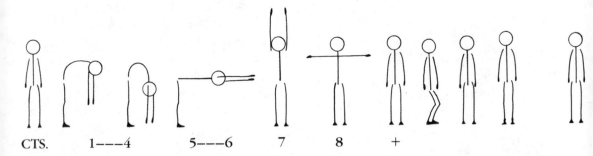

CTS.   1---4   5---6   7   8   +

NOTE: On counts 9-10, be sure to maintain proper alignment with the knees over the toes. Think of each foot as a triangle formed by the big toe, the little toe, and the heel. Do not roll over on either the inner or outer border of the feet. When rising on the balls of the feet (counts 13-14), concentrate on pulling the ankles in toward the center, if they tend to go out at the sides.

12

jazz
choreography
projects
and routines

One way of making the steps and isolations you have learned feel like they are really yours is to use them—put them together in a dance, or choreograph a dance. Any number can play; it is lots of fun and it also makes you see these old steps in a new and individual way. They now feel as though they really belong to you or to the group.

As an instructor, I have always enjoyed seeing the results of these choreography projects, either on the last day or last two days of an 8- or 12-week course in jazz dance. The students seem to enjoy it also. We keep it very flexible; there is a lot of give and take, and much can be learned by everybody involved if you try to keep an open mind to ideas that vary from your own. You see the familiar in a new way. Also, if you keep practicing each new section, and then add it onto the previous section, you will have a segment of a dance routine that you will know quite well and that you will have helped to create.

Following are hints for individual or group choreography using the various steps you have learned. (These can be applied to any other form of dance equally well.) Start by asking yourself questions. If a group is doing the choreography together, you may either ask each person a question in order, and then try whatever that person suggests, go on to the next person with the next question, and so on; or you may wish to discuss it further among yourselves and choose the answer the whole group prefers. But if you have a very talkative group, remember that this should all lead to some action. Make some sort of decision, and get on with it.

jazz choreography projects and routines

1. How large is the group that is involved? Try to be flexible; if the routine is not completed in one session, adapt to any additions or subtractions in the number of people in the group in the next session. This often leads to rather unexpected groupings and formations that might not have been thought of originally. These may be changed again if you so choose.

2. What about "proscenium stage" or "staging in-the-round?" Proscenium is the more usual theater stage, with a wall on three sides and an audience on only one side. In-the-round staging, on the other hand, has to be interesting from all directions, since the audience will be seated all around. The shape of the stage area is often round, especially in large summer stock tents. Small theater groups often use the in-the-round stage area, as do dance companies who must perform in unusual places. Working in-the-round gives one new insights into choreographic formations that would work equally well in proscenium staging; however, one might not think of using these when anticipating an audience on only one side.

3. What music would you like to use? Take into consideration the steps you have learned, and the rhythms of the steps or combinations of steps you might be using. Also, consider the ability of the group and of the individuals in it. (Remember that some persons would do a step slowly, while others do it more quickly in the routine.)

4. Is the routine going to begin with:
   a) Everyone on stage?
   b) Everyone off stage, entering while the music plays?
   c) Some off stage and some on stage?

5. How are the dancers arranged on stage at opening?
   a) Symmetrical arrangements: vertical, horizontal, or diagonal lines, a square, or some other variation?
   b) Unsymmetrical groups in identical or individual poses?

6. Continue asking yourself (if you are doing a solo) or ask the different persons in the group what movement they would like to do next and how many times they would like to do that movement. Consider the following in making your decisions as you prepare the routine.
   a) Use of different levels—low, medium, high.
   b) Use of isolations.
   c) Use of small segments from the combinations learned—take them apart, put them together again in your own way.

d) Vary the formations: lines, circles, groupings, as well as the directional facings of the various individuals.

e) Vary the placement of the dancers on stage (more interesting for audience, too).

f) Vary the dynamics and speed, so there is not a feeling of monotony or sameness throughout.

g) Remember that everyone does not always have to face front at all times. The back and side views are interesting, too.

h) Do movements in place if you have just done a lot of traveling movements.

i) Have a portion of the group do an entire combination that they know well, while the others do either a slower movement in place, body isolations, or hold poses at various levels—high, medium, low. In this way you can make allowances for varying stages of expertise within your group.

j) Have half the group face the back and half face the front, and do the same movement, either all to their right (in which case the group facing front travels to stage right, and the group facing the back, or up stage, travels to stage left); or have them all travel to stage right (then the group facing the back, or up stage, travels to their left). This is good for proscenium staging also.

k) Slow and fast—have one group do a walk combination quickly, going through another line in front of them that is doing the same combination twice as slowly, so that the back horizontal line moves forward, going through the front horizontal line, and ahead of them. In this way you consider the person who can do a step well, but only slowly, and also the one who is more proficient.

l) At some point have each person do a segment of a combination one at a time, one after the other—first person, second person, and so on (A, A', A", A"') or with the entire group doing a different short phrase in between (A, BA', BA", BA"').

m) Use repetition of a dance motif; consider adding a quarter turn before each repetition of the motif.

n) Begin huddled in a group and gradually spread out with individual walks as desired, and then do unison movements.

o) Do a long combination, but have each individual begin on a different count in the music.

jazz choreography projects and routines

p) For more ideas on formations and groups, be aware during your daily activities of the movements and designs around you: the spokes of a wheel, traffic at an intersection, a group of people standing either huddled in a group or by ones or twos.

Following are several routines put together as an end-of-the-course project for beginners' classes under my direction. Some are based on the exact basic steps and combinations, but it is interesting to see what completely different visual effects were achieved. The usage of the steps and the final results were so different in each. The dances are listed by the title of the piece of music used, usually a piece that was a suitable tempo for the majority of the beginning students and for the steps learned by the class. Directions use DSR—down stage right, USL—upstage left, and so on. The steps are not explained in detail, but references are made to previous explanations in this book, unless there are variations in the routine that need precise explanation in this chapter (there are a few of these). In general, the routines stick to what was taught in class.

As you try out your own creative project, remember that most ideas tend to work out in some fashion but if you don't like something, throw it out and start afresh. You don't have to finish it; go as far as you choose, but try to know that amount very well. Also, don't be afraid to change the music if you find it does not work with all the steps. Use something you have utilized when practicing your steps, isolations, and so on, so you are familiar with the piece. Enjoy this project. Sometimes it helps also to visualize a costume you might wear, as though you were actually putting on a show.

If you plan to write out your routine, I recommend using a few simple stick figures, diagrams of movement directions on stage, and abbreviations to greatly speed up the process while making the description clear and concise. Following are abbreviations that many professional dancers have found useful in writing dance routines and that are used in the routines in this chapter.

AST—at the same time	IP—in place
B—back	L—left
b chg—ball change	OH—overhead
C—center	pt—point
CS—center stage	R—right
cts—counts	SL—stage left
DS—down stage	SR—stage right
DSL—down stage left	USL—up stage left
DSR—down stage right	USR—up stage right
F-front	X—times

Photo by Clotilde

jazz routine
(number 12-1)

POOR BOY
Music—Orion 109A, *Giants of Jazz Dance*

Proscenium stage—audience on only one side; for any size group. See number and chapter referred to for specific information regarding steps used in routines. See beginning of this chapter for explanation of abbreviations used.

COUNTS	MOVEMENT

16 cts Introduction, no movement.

32 cts Two lines of dancers:

      1 enters from DSR and moves horizontally across.

      1 line enters from USL and moves horizontally across AST.

4X: 4X: Flat, low level jazz walks (No. 6-4, Chapter 6) with head pecks (shift) F. All start with R ft.

        4X: High level walks with shoulders up and down (No. 6-8, Chapter 6).

All finish up facing F (DS).

32 cts 4X: Quickly, as written here, or 2X only and twice as slow. All start with R ft.

  8 cts: Mambo R, L, grapevine, kick F, rond de jambe en l'air (No. 10-3, Chapter 10).

  8 cts: Reverse.

  8 cts: Reverse.

  8 cts: Reverse.

8 cts All face SR and travel toward SR.

      2X: Low level passé walks, passé, rise on ball of foot, round and arch torso, snaps—2 cts for each passé walk (No. 9-2, Chapter 9).

8 cts 1X: Low level outside turn as follows: step side DS with L ft. (2 cts), then B on R ft., still facing SR, and do outside turn to R (No. 8-1, Chapter 8).

16 cts Repeat the above 16 cts (No. 9-2 and No. 8-1), exactly as before, but finish facing the audience (DS).

64 cts Reverse the above 64 cts, starting with the mambo, then facing SL and traveling toward SL, turning L, and finish facing F (DS).

64 cts	4X: Slowly—F and B lines change places, doing alternately—F line a, then b; B line b, then a.
	a: 8X Kimbos B (2 cts each).
	b: 8X Low level passé walks F with 1 arm swing and snap (2 cts for each passé walk, No. 6-13, Chapter 6).

64 cts	All Together:
	4X: (1X to US, 1X to DS, 1X to US, 1X to DS; see NOTE for No. 10-4, Chapter 10).
	4 cts: Step right, clap hands 2X, AST pt L ft side with L hip out to side, clap hands once (see No. 6-12, Chapter 6).
	8 cts: 2X: Slow high level passé walks with jazz hands and AST do ½ turn R (No. 6-16, Chapter 6).
	4 cts: 3X: Low level twist walks (No. 6-6, Chapter 6).

35 cts	Start to exit. All to SL in 3 groups vertically across. 1st group then pauses then moves; 2nd group pauses then moves; 3rd group pauses longer then moves.
	8 cts: 1st group: 4X: Flat low level walks with head pecks (No. 6-4, Chapter 6).
	4X: High level walks with shoulders up and down (No. 6-8, Chapter 6).
	Then pause.
	8 cts: 2nd group: Catch up with 1st group by doing the same step as in previous 8 cts after the first group stops.
	8 cts: All groups: 1st and 2nd groups: Close up ranks while repeating the same 8 cts of walks.
	3rd group: Now joins 1st and 2nd group in the 8 cts of walks, having paused until now.
	5 cts: All turn a simple turnabout and look back at the audience, while posing individually, as desired, in some jazzy pose.

jazz choreography projects and routines

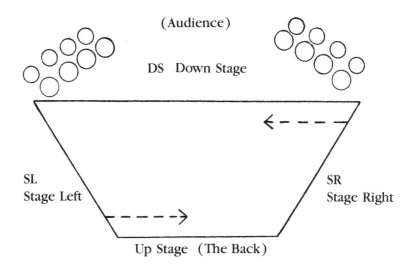

(Audience)

DS   Down Stage

SL
Stage Left

SR
Stage Right

Up Stage   (The Back)

NOTE: If you have learned the steps, combinations, and abbreviations in this book, you should be able to do these movements. They do not contain anything that is not in the book.

jazz routine (number 12-2)

CROCODILE ROCK
Music—Avant No. 120 B, LP, *Jazz Back to Back*

> In-the-round staging; for a large group of 13-25.

COUNTS	MOVEMENT
16 cts (a)	Introduction: large class: 4 groups—A, B, C, D. medium class: 2 groups—A, B.

A and D: 4X: 4X: Flat, low level jazz walks with head pecks (shift), 2 steps in 1 ct (No. 6-4, Chapter 6).

4X: High level walks with shoulders up and down (No. 6-8, Chapter 6).

B and C: 16X: High level walks with jazz hands; 1 ct for each step (No. 6-16, Chapter 6).

A and D move quickly;
B and C move slowly.

64 cts (b)	Mambo Square (see No. 10-4, Chapter 10).	

16 cts: Facing DS
16 cts: Facing SR
16 cts: Facing US
16 cts: Facing SL—one time each way

8 cts (c)   4 cts: 8X Low level twist walks (see No. 6-6, Chapter 6) to a corner, into 4 groups, 1 group in each corner.

4 cts: Individual improvisional isolations with head, shoulder, ribcage, or hips (see Chapter 4).

24 cts (d)   8 cts: Get into a very large circle, or a double circle, if a large group, with skimming step b chg (No. 6-18, Chapter 6).

8 cts: Continue the last step and gradually make the single or double circles tighter and smaller, with arms overlapping over neighbor's arms; all face C of circle.

4 cts: Ribcage isolations, 2X each side (R, R, L, L); these are called doubles.

4 cts: Single ribcage isolations in circle (No. 4-5, Chapter 4).

16 cts (e)   8 cts: 4X: Leg extensions, developees (No. 4-9, Chapter 4) with pt and flex, facing C of circle.

8 cts: All shimmy shoulders; bending F, then coming up with arms OH (No. 4-6, Chapter 4).

16 cts (f)   16X: Low level passé walks to invert the 1 or 2 circles from the previous formation into 2 or 4 straight lines. Do the low level passé walks with the arm swing (No. 6-13, Chapter 6), and even out the number of people in shorter inside lines to equal the longer outside lines, if desired.
DS group start with L ft and R arm.
US group start with R ft and L arm.
All finish by facing SR.

32 cts (g)   8 cts: 1X: 2 low level passé walks, passé, rise, round and arch torso, snaps (No. 9-2, Chapter 9).

8 cts:	All face US; step side on L ft, B on R, and low level outside turn R, step down on R ft (No. 8-1, Chapter 8).	
8 cts:	Face SL; repeat the last 8 cts in this group of steps, starting with L ft.	
8 cts:	Face DS; repeat the second 8 cts in this group of steps; step R and turn L.	
24 cts (h)	24X:	Palm presses toward the ceiling (see No. 5-4, Chapter 5), AST taking small steps, gradually closing the group in, into a tight cluster in the C.

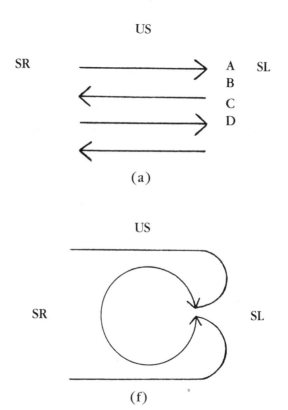

(a)

(f)

NOTE: Look up any of the steps you do not remember well; numbers and chapters are noted in the routines. You will have fun trying out these routines. All the steps and abbreviations are covered in this book. Abbreviations are in this chapter, just before the routines.

jazz routine
(number 12-3)

<u>SOPHISTICATED SWING</u>
<u>Music, Avant LP 120, *Jazz Back to Back*</u>

Proscenium staging, solo, 1 dancer.

COUNTS	MOVEMENT
16 cts (a)	Introduction: on stage in a pose, R arm side, L arm OH, diagonal high side; hold pose.
8 cts (b)	Hip lift: R, C, L, C, R, C, L, C, with knees bent; ft parallel and arms as in pose above (see No. 4-7, Chapter 4).

8 cts (c)

Cts. 1-2:	R shoulder F and B; arms in same position as before for cts 1-8.
Cts. 3-4:	L shoulder F and B.
Cts. 5-6:	R shoulder F and B.
+7:	L shoulder F and B.
+8:	Hip lift, R, L (arms in original pose up to now).

6 cts (d)

1+a2+:	Step R, 2 claps, pt L ft side, clap (No. 6-12, Chapter 6).
3+a4+:	Reverse.
5+ 6+:	Grapevine, R ft B, L ft side, R ft F, and pt L ft side (grapevine No. 7-5, Chapter 7, without kick).

6 cts (e)

7+a8+	
1+a2+	
3+4+	Reverse above 6 cts

4 cts (f)

5+6+	3 low level twist steps, R, L, R, (No. 6-6, Chapter 6).
7+a8+	Step L, 2 claps, pt ft side, clap (No. 6-12, Chapter 6).

4 cts (g)	1 set of camel walks to DS with arm isolation (No. 6-19, Chapter 6).
4 cts (h)	Preparation and low level outside turn: step R, L ft B, turn L, and close ft together (see No. 8-1, Chapter 8).
8 cts (i)	Repeat above 8 cts in same direction.
64 cts (j)	Mambo square: start facing DS, SR, US, SL (No. 10-4, Chapter 10).
4 cts (k)	1 set of camel walks to DS with arm isolation (No. 6-19, Chapter 6).

12 cts (1)	4 cts:	4X:	Flat, low level jazz walks with head pecks (shift) (No. 6-4, Chapter 6).
		4X:	High level walks with shoulders up and down (No. 6-8, Chapter 6).
	4 cts:	Repeat above 4 cts	
	4 cts:	Repeat above 4 cts	
7 cts (m)	To return to SR and same pose as at beginning:		
	2X:	High level twist walks (No. 6-5, Chapter 6), 2 cts for each one.	
	3X:	Low level walks (No. 6-6, Chapter 6).	

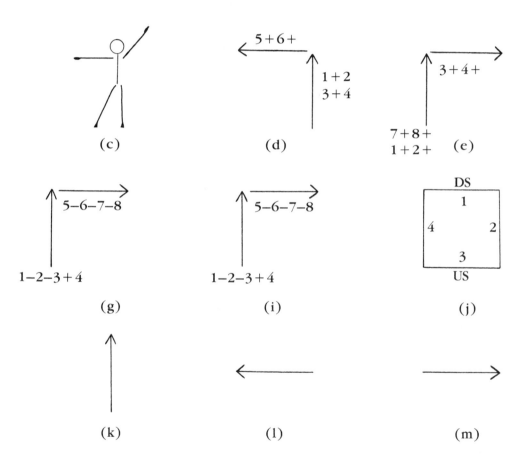

(c)   (d)   (e)

(g)   (i)   (j)

(k)   (l)   (m)

NOTE: The abbreviations used in this routine are the ones usually found in well-written routines and are explained in this chapter just before the routines. The steps are all covered in detail in this book, and they are referred to by the same names throughout the book.

jazz routine
(number 12-4)

SOPHISTICATED SWING
Music—Avant LP 120, *Jazz Back to Back*

In-the-round staging, for three people.

COUNTS	MOVEMENT
8 cts	Introduction, no movement.
16 cts (a)	3 people enter, each from different points of a triangle.

	4X:	2X:	High level passé walks; 2 steps in 2 cts (No. 6-16, Chapter 6).
		3X:	Low level twist walks; 3 steps in 2 cts (No. 6-6, Chapter 6), into a close circle.

16 cts (b) R arm is under neighbor's L arm, extended at sides and overlapping in a circle.

2X:	4 cts:	Ribcage shift R, C, L, C (one ct each position) (No. 4-5, Chapter 4).
	4 cts:	Ribcage shift side 2X each side (R, R, L, L). These are double isolations.

4 cts (c) 4X: Kimbos B and C circle, backing out to enlarge circle, starting with R ft slowly (No. 7-1, Chapter 7).

4 cts (d) 2X: Grapevine and kick F (No. 7-5, Chapter 7), moving circularly starting with R ft first time (2 cts), then L ft second time (2 cts), moving to L then to R.

8 cts (e) 8X: Kimbos backing into a straight line (No. 7-1, Chapter 7).

16 cts (f) 3X: Camel walk with arm isolation (No. 6-19, Chapter 6), into a triangular formation (4 cts each set).
1X: All face C of triangle in 4 cts

COUNTS	MOVEMENT

12 cts (g) 1 at a time:

cts 1-4:	Step side on R ft, step B on L ft and outside turn to L; finish with L arm gesturing to next person at your L and R hand on waist (No. 8-1, Chapter 8).
cts 5-8:	Next person goes.
cts 9-12:	Third person goes.

16 cts (h) 8X: Low level passé walks (No. 6-7, Chapter 6), clockwise.
8X: Low level walks into a straight line.

32 cts (i)   Fugally (one starting after the other, not all together), do the low level passé walk, rise on ball of ft and round and arch torso, and so on (No. 9-2, Chapter 9), 4 cts for one time. All to SL as if to exit.

        1st person: Starts and does it 4X and steps and pauses.
        2nd person: Waits 2X and does it 4X and steps and
                  pauses.
        3rd person: Waits 4X and does it 4X.

16 cts (j)   2 cts: 1X: All about face and face SR.
          12 cts: 3X: 4X: Flat low level jazz walk (No. 6-4, Chapter 6), with head pecks, shift; 1 ct for 2 steps.
                               4X: High level walks (No. 6-8, Chapter 6), with shoulders up and down, to return to CS (1 ct for 2 steps).
          2 cts: 1X: All finish in any pose facing any direction on last chord of music.

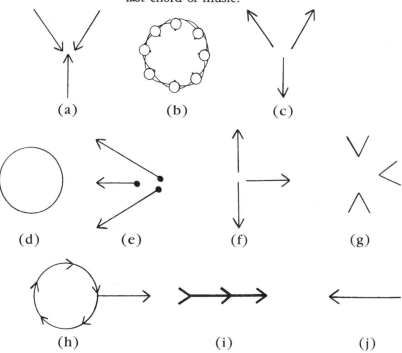

NOTE: You have had all these steps and abbreviations previously in this book. If you cannot figure out the routine, look up the steps you may not remember and go slowly. Practice 8 counts, then 8 more; then do 16 cts and add 8 more, and so on until you know the whole routine.

Photo by Clotilde

13 discography

This chapter contains a list of records suitable for practicing jazz dance. These include some records I have used for classroom purposes and many that I have simply enjoyed listening to. There are innumerable others that would be equally good for jazz dance; you can probably think of several favorite pieces of your own. The records on this list can be purchased or ordered from your local music store; the ones made specifically for dance classes can be ordered from some of the dealers in dance supplies who handle dance records, such as Herbet's Dancewear in New York City. Check your classified phone book for addresses.

Giants of Jazz Dance (Orion, LP, 109)

Rich Man's Frug	The Happening
The Swinger	Big Spender
Poor Boy	Jazzerina
Gonnella	

Think Jazz—Gus (Orion, LP, 105)

Think Jazz Cha Cha	Chicago
Cuban Drums	Drum Rock
Swingin Drums	Drum Beguine

Jazz Express (Avant Records, LP, 121)

Boogie Woogie Bugle Boy	Down At Papa Joes
Space Race	Soul Makossa
Lullaby of Broadway	Varsity Drag

Dave Brubeck At Storyville: 1954 (Columbia, LP, CL 590)

On the Alamo	Gone With the Wind
Don't Worry 'Bout Me	When You're Smiling
Here Lies Love	Back Bay Blues

Louis Armstrong Plays W. C. Handy (Columbia, LP, CL 591)

St. Louis Blues	Aunt Hagar's Blues
Beale Street Blues	Ole Miss
Chantez-Les Bas	Hesitating Blues

The Roaring 20's (Coronet Records, CXS-2)

Varsity Drag	Ballin' the Jack
Dixie	Goody, Goody
Deep River	Give My Regards to Broadway

Jazz At Columbia—Dixieland (Columbia, LP, CB 8)

Blues	Fidgety Feet
Ace in the Hole	Ain't Misbehavin'
High Society	Oh, Didn't He Ramble
Jazz Me Blues	Original Dixieland One Step
Bill Bailey	Ole Miss

I Love Movies—Michel Legrand (Columbia, LP, CL 1178)

The Third Man Theme	River of No Return
Sonny Boy	Carioca

Mr. Music—Al Cohn (RCA Victor, LP, LJM 1024)

Something for Lisa	Move
La Ronde	This Reminds Me of You
Breakfast With Joe	Cohn My Way

Saturday Night Mood (Columbia, LP, CL 599)

Blue Skies
The Little White Duck
Sunday

Daddy
Planters Punch

Le Grand Jazz—Michel Legrand—Miles Davis (Columbia, LP, CL 1250)

Django
Wild Man Blues
'Round Midnight

Stompin' at the Savoy
Rosetta

Jazz With Luigi (Hoctor, LP 3063)

Don't Worry About It
Little Boy Blue
The Swinger

Someone and I Do
Laughing Boy
Corner of the Moon

The Sting—Scott Joplin, movie using his music (MCA 2040)

Afro-American Jazz Dance (Orion, LP 115)

Apollo
White Sound

Lennox
Black Sound

The Ragtime Years—Irving Berlin—Mox Morath (Vanguard, LP, VSD 79346)

Everything in America
   Is Ragtime
Mr. Jazz Himself

Let Me Sing and I'm Happy
The Grizzly Bear

Follies (Statler, LP 1183)

The Walk
Get Down

Mockingbird
Papa's Got a Brand New Bag

Music Hall (Statler, LP 1181)

Riviera Rage

Peppermint Twist

Jazz Back to Back (Avant, LP 120)

Crocodile Rock
The Stripper

Outa Space
Frankie and Johnny

discography

Music Man (Capital Records, SW-990, original Broadway cast

> Book, music, lyrics—Meredith Wilson (1957)
> Choreographer—Oona White
> (Original stage show included a marvelous train scene
> choreography.)

Hello Dolly (Victor, LSOD-1087-RE, original Broadway cast)

> Music—Jerry Herman; lyrics—Michael Stewart (1964)
> Choreography—Gower Champion
> (Original Broadway stage show had delightful scene with waiters
> dancing.)

Damn Yankees (RCA Victor, LSO—102, original Broadway cast)

> Music and lyrics—Richard Adler and Jerry Ross (1955)
> Choreography—Bob Fosse
> (Original stage show had a mixture of baseball and modern jazz,
> creating great dance effects.)

Guys and Dolls (Decca 79023, original Broadway cast)

> Music and lyrics—Frank Loesser based on a story by Damon
> Runyon (1950)
> Choreography—Michael Kidd
> (Original stage show included a remarkable crap shooters dance
> number as well as calypso jazz and Times Square atmosphere.)

Chorus Line (Columbia, PS-33581, original Broadway cast)

> Music—Marvin Hamlisch; lyrics—Edward Kleban (1975)
> Choreographed and directed by Michael Bennet
> (Original stage show included tap and jazz and made each
> member of the auditioning chorus stand out as a human being
> with a personality of his or her own.)

Bye Bye Birdie (Columbia, KOS-2025, original Broadway cast)

> Music—Charles Strouse; lyrics—Lee Adams (1960)
> Choreography—Gower Champion
> (Original stage show included rock and fad dances and a telephone
> booth dance number.)

Sweet Charity (Columbia, KOS-2900, original Broadway cast)

> Music—Cy Coleman; lyrics—Dorothy Fields (1966)
> Choreography—Bob Fosse

(Original stage show included fad dances of the rock type—frug, monkey, and a typewriter dance).

Godspell (Arista AB 4001, original Broadway cast)

Music and lyrics—Stephen Schwartz (1971)
(Improvisational-type dance movement performed in the original stage show under the direction of John-Michael Tebelak).

Any of the top hits of the week that you like with a jazzy beat— listen to the radio or watch TV.

I'M COMING OUT (Motown 1491) Diana Ross
DREAMING (EM:AMERICA) Cliff Richards

bibliography

Jazz Dance

Audy, Robert, *Jazz Dancing*. New York: Random House, 1978.

Cayou, Dolores Kirton, *Modern Jazz Dance*. Palo Alto, Calif.: National Press Books, 1971.

Czompo, Ann L., *Recreational Jazz Dance*. New York: Ann L. Czompo, 1971.

Dance Masters of America, *Jazz Syllabus*, 1978.

Dunning, Jennifer, "High Stepping Into Stardom," *New York Times*, Arts and Leisure Section, April 2, 1976, p. 1.

Emery, Lynne Fauley, *Black Dance in the United States From 1619 to 1970*. Palo Alto, Calif.: National Press Books, 1972.

Fischer-Munstermann, Uta, *Jazz Dance and Jazz Gymnastics Including Disco Dancing*. New York: Sterling Publishing, 1978.

Giordano, Gus, *Anthology of American Jazz Dance*. Evanston, Ill.: Orion Publishing, 1975.

Kerr, Walter, "'Dancin' Needs More than Dancing." *New York Times*, Section II, April 9, 1978, p. 5.

Panasie, Hugues, "Le Jazz et La Danse." *Formes et Couleurs*. Paris, France, number 4, 1948, tenth year.

Sabatine, Jean, *Technique and Styles of Jazz Dance*. Waldwick, N.J.: Hoctor Dance Records, 1969.

Stearns, Marshall, and Stearns, Jean, *Jazz Dance*. New York: Macmillan, 1968.

Todd, Arthur, "Negro American Theater Dance." *Dance Magazine*. November 1950, pp. 21, 33.

Traguth, Fred, *Modern Jazz Dance*. Bonn, W. Germany: Dance Motion Press, 1978.

Ballet

Balanchine, George, *Complete Stories of the Great Ballet.* New York: Doubleday, 1954.

Guillet, Genevieve, and Prudhommeau, Germaine, *The Book of Ballet* Englewood Cliffs, N.J.:Prentice-Hall, Inc., 1976.

Karsavina, Tamara, *Classical Ballet: The Flow of Movement.* New York: Macmillan, 1963.

Stuart, Muriel, *The Classical Ballet: Basic Technique and Terminology.* New York: Knopf, 1962.

Vaganova, Agrippina, *Fundamentals of the Classic Dance.* New York: Dover, 1971.

General Dance

Berger, Melvin, *The World of Dance.* New York: Phillips, 1978.

De Mille, Agnes, *The Book of the Dance.* New York: Golden Press, 1963.

Hering, Doris, ed., *25 Years of American Dance.* New York: Rudolph Orthwine, 1951.

Kraus, Richard, *History of Dance.* Englewood Cliffs, N.J.: Prentice-Hall, Inc., 1969.

Reynolds, Nancy, ed., *The Dance Catalog.* New York: Harmony Books, 1979.

Terry, Walter, and Renners, Jack, *100 Years of Dance Posters.* New York: Darien House, 1975.

Weill, Alain, *100 Years of Posters of the Folies Bergeres and Music Halls of Paris.* New York: Images Graphiques, 1978.

Indian Dance

Devi, Ragine, *Dance Dialects of India.* Delphi, India: Vikas Publications, 1972.

Hughes, Russell Meriwither, *The Gesture Language of the Hindu Dance/La Meri.* New York: Arno Press, 1979.

Modern Dance

Cheney, Gay, and Strader, Janet, *Modern Dance.* Boston: Allyn and Bacon, 1969.

Gray, Miriam, ed., *Focus on Dance V, Composition.* Washington, D.C.: American Assn. for Health, Phys. Ed. and Recreation, 1969.

McDonagh, Don, *The Rise and Fall and Rise of Modern Dance.* New York: NAL, 1970

Mazo, Joseph, *Prime Movers, the Makers of Modern Dance in America.* New York: William Morrow, 1977.

Penrod, James, and Plastino, Janice Gudde, *The Dancer Prepares, Modern Dance for Beginners,* 2nd ed. Palo Alto, Calif.: Mayfield Publishing, 1980.

Social and Folk Dancing

Bonomo, Joe, *Improve Your Dancing.* New York: Bonomo Culture Institute, 1953, 1962.

Buckman, Peter, *Let's Dance, Social Ballroom and Folk Dancing.* New York: Paddington Press, 1978.

McDonagh, Don, *Dance Fever.* New York: Random House, 1979.

Monte, John, and Lawrence, Bobie. *The Fred Astaire Dance Book.* New York: Simon and Schuster, 1978.

Stoop, Norma Mclain, "Telescoping Time," *Dance Magazine,* March 1980, pp. 85, 86.

Tap Dance

Ames, Jerry, and Siegelman, Jim, *The Book of Tap.* New York: David McKay, 1977.

Audy, Robert, *Tap Dancing—How to Teach Yourself.* New York: Random House, 1976.

Hungerford, Mary Jane, *History of Tap Dancing.* Englewood Cliffs, N.J.: Prentice-Hall, Inc., 1939.

Nash, Barbara, *Tap Dance.* Dubuque, Iowa: Wm. C. Brown, 1969.

Shipley, Glenn, *Modern Tap Dictionary.* Los Angeles: Action Marketing Group, 1976.

Film

Crowther, Bosley, *Reruns 50 Memorable Films.* New York: Putnam, 1978.

Productions

Ellfeldt, Lois, and Carnes, Edwin, *Dance Production Handbook, or Later Is Too Late.* Palo Alto, Calif.: National Press Books, 1971.

McCandles, Stanley, *A Method of Lighting the Stage.* New York: Theatre Arts Books, 1958.

Melcer, Fannie Helen, *Staging the Dance.* Dubuque, Iowa: Wm. C. Brown, 1955.